The American Journalists

THE NEWSPAPER PRESS
OF CHARLESTON, S. C.

William L. King

ARNO
&
The New York Times

Collection Created and Selected
by Charles Gregg of Gregg Press

Reprint edition 1970 by Arno Press Inc.

LC# 72-125701
ISBN 0-405-01680-8

The American Journalists
ISBN for complete set: 0-405-01650-6

Reprinted from a copy in
The Columbia University Library

Manufactured in the United States of America

THE

NEWSPAPER PRESS

OF

CHARLESTON, S. C.

A Chronological and Biographical History,
Embracing a period of One Hundred
and Forty Years.

BY

WILLIAM L. KING.

De dictis factisque memoratu dignis.

CHARLESTON, S. C.:

EDWARD PERRY, (BOOK PRESS) 149 MEETING STREET.

1872.

ARCHIBALD EDWARD MILLER.

To you, sir, the only surviving typographer of the past century, now living in this City, I inscribe this work. As you are aware, it is the only history of the rise and progress of the newspaper press of Charleston, S. C. I desire to prefix your name to this *brochure*, for two reasons. First, as an acknowledgment of the kindness you have ever evinced towards the craft. Secondly, because through the course of your long life, you have been that exemplar of rectitude to whom they of the *stick* and *rule*, will point in the future, as they have in the past, with pride and honor.

Very truly, yours,

WILLIAM L. KING.

Charleston, S. C., 1872.

PREFACE.

The attention of the reader is invited to the following pages, indited without pretentious or special claim to literary merit. The author's object was solely to prevent local, historical facts from passing into oblivion, or becoming apocryphal.

To those, therefore, who love to look back upon the past, through a long vista of nearly a century and a half, a veritable record of events, together with such mutations in their order of succession as go to form a faithful chronological history of the newspaper press of Charleston, will, perhaps, command that consideration, which otherwise, could only be claimed through richness of diction, or elegance of style.

The author is among those who believe in the sentiment so felicitously expressed by D'ISRAELI : " To preserve the past, is half of immortality."

CONTENTS.

CHAPTER I.

CHAPTER II.

CHAPTER III.

CHAPTER VIII.

CHAPTER IX.

CHAPTER X.

CHAPTER XI.

CHAPTER XII.

CHAPTER XIII.

CHAPTER XIV.

CHAPTER XV.

CHAPTER XVI.

CHAPTER XVII.

CHAPTER XVIII.

CHAPTER XIX.

THE NEWSPAPER PRESS.

"Hail Printing, Hail! thou thrice illustrious Art!
Which clear'd the Head, and which reform'd the Heart,
Bless'd with new Light, a superstitious age,
And purg'd the Relics of barbarick Rage;
From thee celestial Streams of Learning flow,
And to thy Pow'r we pure Religion owe."

[REV'D. DR. BIRCH.]

CHAPTER I.

THE ART OF PRINTING—CLAIMS OF INVENTORS—ITS BE-
NEFICENT INFLUENCES—THE AUTHOR OF THIS BROCHURE
A PRINTER—THE WORD "NEWS" FIGURATIVELY INTER-
PRETED—NEWSPAPERS—THEIR ORIGIN IN ENGLAND—
ADVERTISING AND EDITING IN EARLY TIMES—SOCIAL
ORGANIZATION OF THE PRESS RECOMMENDED—WANT OF
A PROPER HISTORY OF OUR CITY PRESS—THIS THE FIRST
WRITTEN—ELEAZER PHILLIPS THE FIRST PRINTER IN
THE COLONY—DIFFICULTIES ATTENDING THIS COMPILA-
TION.

FAMOUS among the inventive arts stands Printing. Its
first appearance, between the years 1422 and 1436, was a
new era in civilization. It casts around mankind, on every
side, beneficent influences. Revelation and science are
taught by it to wear the garb, and speak the language of
unperverted judgment.

1

It does not clearly appear to whom we are indebted for this all-controlling art. The city of Mentz, situated on the Rhine, just below its confluence with the Main, and the rich and populous city of Haërlem, the one in Germany, and the other on the river Sparen, in Holland, have long contended for the priority of its invention. Though the popular voice is in favor of Mentz, yet HADRIANUS JUNIUS names Haërlem as the birth-place of this noble art.

The claim of individual invention seems, after sifting the most authentic data, to be equally balanced between JOHN GUTTENBURG, a knight and citizen, and JOHANN FAUST, both of the former city, and LAURENTIUS VILLA, sometimes called LAWRENCE JANSZOON KOSTER, once an alderman of the latter place.

The result of this invention is most happy. The very power which it conveys is attended with peculiar pleasure, such as few other arts in equal measure impart. The compositor at his *case* can complacently consider himself the disseminator of intelligence to legions, and maintains a secret, yet personal influence, over a boundless sphere. He feels also, that he is serving the cause of mankind, and his labor becomes his pleasure.

In the autumn of 1843, the author, at the instance of his father, WM. S. KING, entered as an apprentice in the office of *The Charleston Courier*, a journal then, as now, owned by Messrs. A. S. WILLINGTON & Co. The business management and assistant editorship of this daily was, for many years, committed to his father, and the apprenticeship was during its continuance under his supervision.

To many of the craft in this city, this information is unnecessary, yet it is mentioned to show that however distrustful the author may feel of his ability to do justice to the work now undertaken, he has at least the merit of possessing, to some extent, the experience which may be regarded

as indispensable to its proper and practical exposition. Indeed, he would have preferred one riper in years, who had
been at the *case* longer than himself, to have undertaken a
subject which has been so long neglected. He assumes
the task without any apprehensions of its labor, and feels
that he will be stimulated in its performance by the con-
viction that it is a pleasurable duty.

Many persons read newspapers without considering the
importance of the word "News," or even interpreting,
figuratively, the import which is attached to the word. In
the first place, *news* come from all quarters of the globe,
and so the constituent letters of the word itself demon-
strates, viz: N.E.W.S.—North, East, West and South.
No language furnishing a word more expressive. Again,
when further considered, these cardinal letters recommend
to us the practice of the four following virtues : Nobleness
in our thoughts, Equity in our dealings, Wisdom in our
conduct, Sobriety in our lives.

The newspaper of to-day is, in every respect, far in advance of what it was a half century ago. More especially
does it differ in point of management. This medium has
an unlimited agency in modern society, for circulating information respecting the whole range of human concerns,
from the affairs of nations, and the researches of science, to
the minutest interests of individuals. In its editorial and
general conduct there is perceptible, also, an increased fear-
lessness. Things which in the time of Junius* would have

---

* These celebrated letters of "Junius" were prepared for "The Public Advertiser," published in London. The Advertiser was published for forty
years, by Henry Sampson Woodfall, who died in London 12th September,
1805, aged 67 years. From a paper published in the year 1788, is taken the
following curious political anecdote of Garrick and Junius:

"At the close of Junius's political warfare, Mr. Garrick received a note in
his dressing-room from the present Mr. Henry Sampson Woodfall, informing him that the Public Advertiser of that day contained the last letter that
would be published by that very celebrated writer. Convinced that the

set London agog, and thoughts not less eloquent than were written in those sixty-nine letters, now pass almost daily without especial notice. So, too, with the mechanical operations of the newspaper. They have reached a perfection calculated to astonish those who may examine its history.

In England, the value of newspapers was first appreciated in the solid and frugal policy of Lord CECIL WILLIAM BURLEIGH, who, for nearly forty years, was the most successful Minister of Queen ELIZABETH. For, when his country, during the reign of that Queen, was threatened by Spain with invasion, he availed himself of their use and through them informed the people of the enemy's movements. The designs of his adversaries were thus frequently overthrown.

But the importance of these printed sheets, then only occasionally issued, was not thoroughly understood, until the beginning of the wars which occurred between CHARLES the First and his Parliament, consequent upon the main-

---

tidings of such an event would be highly acceptable at Buckingham-House, Mr. Garrick instantly wrote to Mr. Ramus, then royal factotum, as follows :

My dear Ramus, Junius writes no more !

Your's, ever truly, D. G."

" Mr. Ramus, as may be supposed, lost not a moment's time in conveying this agreeable intelligence to the Sovereign's ear, and that with the utmost privacy : notwithstanding which, Mr. Garrick, to his unspeakable astonishment, received the following letter the next day, in the identical handwriting of Junius : for which extraordinary circumstance he was unable to account to the day of his death.

COPY.

MONDAY.

Sir,

" Your prudential habits might have prevented you from becoming the unnecessary intelligencer of my designs. I stood not in need of your offices to proclaim my intentions. Probably the measure was suggested by some personal vanity : in that case you shall not long remain ungratified : for, having done with the baneful politics of Princes, I have now full leisure to descend to the mimic Monarchs of the stage.

JUNIUS."

tenance of rights which encroached on royal prerogatives. Then began that competition among newspaper writers, which has since been carried to a most remarkable extent. The rapid and wide publicity given to whatever was printed, soon suggested to individuals a way, not only to make their talents apparent, but to have their wishes fashioned into and expressed by advertisements.

The editor of a journal formerly, was its printer and publisher; something more, he was a sort of sponsor for the accuracy of its advertising customers. The sleep of the editor of the present day, did he undertake to vouch for all of the advertisements which appear in the columns of his paper, would not be a repose on a bed of roses.

The first consideration to be looked to, in advancing the newspaper business, is the necessity among proprietors and editors of a close social organization. This combination is the primary secret of success, and was so regarded by the proprietors and editors of our daily papers, who stood in former years as a host within themselves. This social existence appears to have expired with its projectors, and its principles seem to have been entombed with them when they were gathered to their fathers.

> "The treasures of antiquity laid up
> In old historic rolls, I opened,"

and in opening them, find it refreshing to recall the characteristics of those able editorial workers who constituted the old Charleston press. Of these, but few now survive.

Neither in the "Reminiscences of South Carolina," by E. S. THOMAS, who but casually refers to the newspaper press, nor in the valuable works of RAMSAY, FRASER or DALCHO, (the latter in early life an editor,) can there be found any record of the Press of Charleston. That octogenarian editor, JACOB N. CARDOZO, in his "Reminiscen-

ces," gives but a brief *resumé* of the Press of Charleston.
In this particular the historians of our craft here seemed at
least to have been remiss.

ISAIAH THOMAS, LL. D., of Massachusetts, one of the
most eminent of American printers, in his "History of
Printing in America," has paid great attention to the subject of newspapers in general.   To ELEAZER PHILLIPS, he
gives the credit of having been, as early as 1730, the "first
printer to his Majesty," but does not say that he published
the first newspaper in the Colony.   THOMAS does not even
refer to, nor does he seem to have possessed that information
in regard to the advent of the press, which the author has
gathered from the records of that exceedingly valuable institution—the Charleston Library Society,* the shelves of
which are peculiarly rich in collections of costly, rare, and
old books.   Among those noted for their antiquity, are
"MARTIAEL's Epigrams," published in Venice, in 1491;
"The second folio edition of WILLIAM SHAKSPEARE's Com-
edies, Histories and Tragedies."   This edition† was printed
in London in 1632, by THOS. COTE, for ROBERT ALLOT, and
"sold at the figure of the Blacke Beare, in St. Paul's
Church Yard."

---

*Shecut, page 40: "Seventeen gentlemen obtained in the year 1754, an act
of incorporation, by which they were known and distinguished as the
'Charleston Library Society.'"

†At a sale in New York city, a few years ago, a copy of the first edition of
this work was "knocked down" for the sum of $127.   Both of the works
mentioned as being in the Library, are in a remarkably complete state of
preservation.

CHAPTER II.

FROM information, carefully gathered, it appears that
the first newspaper published in "Charlestown," after its
permanent settlement* on this side of the Ashley, which
was in 1680, was "*The South Carolina Gazette*, which contains the freshest advices, Foreign and Domestick." The
leader had as a caption this motto, taken from the lines
of HORACE:

> "Omne tulit punctum; qui miscuit utile dulci,
> Lectorem delectando, pariterque monendo."

At the conclusion of the leader or introductory article,

---

* In the exact date of the abandonment of the settlement known as "Old
Town," which was "by a formal command of the proprietors," there is a
discrepancy; authorities, however, predominate in favor of 1680. In all
probability, the transfer from "Old Town" to "Oyster Point," was made
early in that year.

which was signed "Philo-Carolinensis," there were the following verses, dedicated "To all whom it may concern to know me :"

> "I'm not High-Church, nor Low-Church, nor Tory nor Whig,
> No flatt'ring young Coxcomb, nor formal old Prig.
> Not eternally talking, nor silently quaint,
> No profligate sinner, no pragmatical Saint.
> I'm not vain of my judgment, nor pinn'd on a Sleeve,
> Nor implicitly any Thing can I believe.
> To sift Truth from all Rubbish, I do what I can,
> And, God knows, if I err—I'm a fallible man.
> I can laugh at a Jest, if not crack'd out of Time,
> And excuse a mistake, tho' not flatter a Crime.
> Any Faults of my Friends I would scorn to expose,
> And detest private scandal, tho' cast on my Foes.
> I put none to the Blush, on whatever pretence,
> For immodesty shocks both good Breeding and Sense.
> No Man's Person I hate, though his Conduct I blame,
> I can sensure a Vice, without stabbing a name.
> To amend—not reproach—is the Bent of my Mind,
> A Reproof is half lost, when ill nature is join'd.
> Where Merit appears, tho' in Rags, I respect it,
> And plead Virtue's Cause, should the whole World reject it.
> Cool Reason I bow to, wheresoever 'tis found,
> And rejoice when sound Learning with favour is crown'd.
> To no Party a Slave, in no Squabbles I join,
> Nor damn the Opinion that differs from mine.
> Evil Tongues I condemn, no mob Treasons I sing,
> I dote on my Country, and am Liege to my King.
> Tho' length of Days I desire, yet with my last Breath,
> I'm in hopes to betray no mean Dreadings of Death.
> And as to the Path after Death to be Trod,
> I rely on the Will of a merciful God."

THOMAS WHITMARSH arrived in "Charlestown" early in 1731, and was the publisher of the *Gazette*. WHITMARSH took this step with much fear and trembling, and with much foreboding of failure. This feeling was expressed by repeated appeals, and editorial notices. The *Gazette* was eleven and a half inches in length, seven in width, containing eight columns, two to a page. It was put in circulation on "Saturday, January 8, 1731–2," and issued weekly from the "sign of the table-clock, on the Bay, where advertisements are taken in."* The *Gazette* was supplied at £3 á year. Town subscribers were requested to send for their papers every Saturday, by 3 o'clock ; papers for the country subscribers were kept at the office.

GEORGE WEBB and ELEAZER PHILLIPS, jr.,† two other printers, arrived in " Charlestown" about the time THOS. WHITMARSH came, induced hither by encouragement held out by the Governor in Council, and by the Assembly of the Province. The first movement to establish printing in what was then the Colony, was by Council, in December, 1722. In January, 1724, and in May, 1731, movements were again made to have a printer settle in the Colony. That no printing was done in the Colony prior to 1731 is

---

* Thomas and Ramsay assert that "Newspapers were first published in South Carolina, in or about 1730, by Lewis Timothy." Shecut, chapter iii, page 41-2—"The first newspaper printed in the Colony, was one at Charlestown, sometime in the year 1730. The venerable Josiah Smith, who has preserved files of the first and second numbers of newspapers printed in Charlestown, has, within the past year (1819), presented them to the Charleston Library Society." These files are now in the Library, and they are the oldest Colonial newspapers in that repository ; they bear Josiah Smith's autograph. The first edition is dated January 8, 1731-2. Professor Wm. J. Rivers, of the South Carolina College, brought to our attention in a publication of his, in the September number of Russell's Magazine for 1858, a few facts about the introduction of printing into South Carolina. He gathered them from the manuscript records in the State House, at Columbia. In that paper, Professor Rivers questions the statement of the above historians. He says : " If this was the case, why did the Legislature make or renew their appropriation on 21st May, 1731, for the encouragement of a printer to settle here ?" " If printing," he adds, " was introduced in 1730, the Legislature seem not to have been aware of it."

† Eleazer Phillips, jr., died in July, 1732. His father, who was a bookseller, advertised nearly two years after, in the Gazette for a settlement of all debts due himself or the estate of his son, for news, printing, &c. Special mention is made of subscriptions due Eleazer Phillips, jr., for six months of the South Carolina Weekly Journal, a paper which is not named in any of the early records of the press, and of which no other trace can be found. If such a paper did exist, it must either have preceded the Gazette, or been contemporary with it. The Gazette has been commonly regarded as not only the first in time, but for many years, the only newspaper issued in the Town or.Province.

proven by the subjoined quotation from Council Journal, No. 5, page 86, in the State House, at Columbia:

May 21st, 1730. The following was sent to the Lower House:

"We take this opportunity to acquaint you that His "Excellency has informed us that His Majesty, out of his "great goodness to this Province, will be pleased to print "our laws at his own charge, and send over as many "copies as may be necessary. Therefore, recommend this "matter to you, that a copy may be provided of such laws "as are necessary to be printed, that they may be sent "to Great Britain as soon as possible."

It is established that one press was put to work in the Colony as early as 1731, and this fact is authenticated by the publication of several pamphlets, the title pages of which are marked of that date; and a further corroboration is found in references contained in *The South Carolina Gazette*, of the year following; and further, from mention made in the Council Journals now in the State House at Columbia, in manuscript.

The *foreign* advices in the first number of the *Gazette*, tell that "the Charter appointing Trustees for establishing "the Colony of Georgia, in America, is passed 'the Broad "Seal,' and that the Right Honorable the Lord PERCIVAL, "being by the Charter appointed President the 14th in- "stant, he took the oath for the faithful discharge of his "Trust, before the Right Honorable the Lord Chief Jus- "tice, Baron of the Exchequer."

The edition of January 20th, 1732, states: "Saturday "night came to an anchor off our bar, a ship with about "120 people for settling the new Colony of Georgia, in "which was JAMES OGLETHORPE, Esquire, who came ashore "that night, and was extremely well received by His Ex- "cellency, our Governor; the next morning he went on

" board, and the ship sailed for Port Royal ; and we hear
" there are two more ships with people (which will make
" the number 500,) expected daily."

The settling of Georgia was begun in this way : JAMES
OGLETHORPE, at the age of 30, being then a member
of Parliament, obtained the appointment of a legislative commission to inquire into " the state of debtor-pris-
oners in England." The report of that commission, in
the year 1729, set forth so much suffering and oppression,
that OGLETHORPE's proposition to found a Colony in America, was adopted by the British Parliament. With this
Colony, OGLETHORPE designed to establish a settlement,
which should also be an " asylum for the persecuted Pro-
testants of France, Germany and Switzerland, and even,
through them, of converting the Indian tribes to Christianity." The Royal Charter, incorporating the Colony for
twenty-one years, was obtained in 1732. OGLETHORPE,
besides being a philanthropist, was a warrior, and served
with distinction under Prince EUGENE, in his campaign
against the Turks.

An account of the progress of this first Colony, is given
in the issue of the 17th March, 1733.

The *domestic* information in the *Gazette* is, " one day
" last week, one RICHARD BIRMINGHAM, belonging to his
" Majesty's ship Shoreham, was drowned in Wappoo Creek,
" over against Colonel LUCAS' plantation, by endeavoring
" to get the grappling up."

Another piece of *domestic* information, as stated in the
Gazette of the 27th January, 1733, was to this end : " On
" Saturday last, a negro fellow belonging to Mr. ISAAC
" MAZYCK, Sr., pull'd a young lad off his horse on the
" Broad Path, and rode away with the horse and bags
" thereon, in which there were clothes of value. He was
" taken on Sunday ; on Monday brought to Town, tried

"and condemned; on the next day, about noon, he was "hanged."

The office of the *Gazette* was removed at the end of March, 1732, to the residence of Mr. HUGH EVANS, tailor, in Church Street, within a few doors of the Secretary's office,* and the paper appeared on the morning of the 1st April.

From the above, it is apparent that full half a century had elapsed after the settlement of "Charlestown" before the first public journal was established. South Carolina was the fifth Colony in which a newspaper was published.

It may be here properly mentioned, that the pioneer of the American Press was the *News-Letter*,† which was printed in Pudding Lane, Boston, Massachusetts, by JOHN CAMPBELL. Its first issue was from "Monday, April 17, to Monday, April 24, 1704." It was printed on paper nine inches in length and six inches in width—pica type. The oldest of the American weekly papers now extant, is the *Newport Mercury*, established by BENJAMIN FRANKLIN, A. D. 1758. That, at the head of daily newspapers, in point of age, is the *North American and United States Gazette*, of Philadelphia. It is the direct successor of the *Pennsylvania Packet and the General Advertiser*, first issued October 28, 1771.

To recur. The advertisements in the early papers of

---

*The Secretary's office was then located on the east side of Church Street, between the streets now known as Elliott and Tradd. John Hamerton was the Secretary; he was also "Receiver General to his Majesty."

† The edition of the News-Letter, published for the week, from May 22 to May 29, 1710, contains but one advertisement, viz.: "Advertisement—Two negro women, one aged about 25, and the other about 30 years old, to be sold by Mr. Wm. Clark, Junior, merchant, to be seen at his house, Common Street, Boston." It is interesting to learn, at this time, that the first and only newspaper printed in New England, one hundred and sixty years ago, contained a solitary advertisement, and that was—offering two human beings for sale.

South Carolina were limited, and were devoted more particularly to the settlement of estates, official notices and estrays, etc., than to any regular commercial publicity. In these early papers will be seen strong indications of the lively interest and participation taken in the slave trade, for the supply of Charleston, which was afterwards continued on the part of our little sister State, Rhode Island. A considerable portion of the shipping reported in 1732, as engaged in the Charleston trade, is credited to Rhode Island.

The value of the investments in commerce and business generally, with its increased trade, induced a correspondence, in the year 1733, on the question of insurance. The resident merchants of "Charlestown" desired to be underwritten from the offices of London and Bristol, the most frequented ports of the "Mother Country;" but the request was declined, on the ground that no charter then existing permitted such risks. The city was thus left to its own resources, and in four years after, the residents organized a mutual voluntary insurance association. Some other attempts seem to have been made in 1732 to organize these associations, but without any definite result. The largest capitals were invested in ways that could be protected, and it was property in the city that desired guarantees.

Other lines of inquiry and incidental research are supplied by the gazettes, as to the subjects, courses and modes of trade, occupations, manners, habits, etc., of the growing and struggling city, which was for years threatened by the sea itself, and by enemies from the sea, on one side, and on the other by savages and European foes.

THOMAS WHITMARSH continued to be the printer of *The South Carolina Gazette* until his course was arrested by death, which was from yellow or strangers' fever, in

2

the summer of 1733. The paper was continued in his name, and in the last number, to which the name of WHITMARSH is affixed, is that from September 1 to September 8, 1733. This appeal is made in the edition dated August 4 to August 11, 1733, with the view of closing up the affairs of the first publisher—

"Gentlemen: It is but a little to each of you, tho' it "will be a considerable sum to me; and lying in many "hands wide from each other, (according to the Nature of "our Business,) it is highly inconvenient, and scarce practi- "cable for me to call upon every one; I shall, therefore, "think myself particularly obliged, and take it very kind "of those who are mindful to send or bring it in without "further notice."

Nothing beyond this is known of the publisher, WHITMARSH.

LEWIS TIMOTHY, the successor of WHITMARSH, was a French refugee; he went to Holland, and from thence to "Charlestown," early in 1733. In February of the same year he became the proprietor and editor of the *Gazette*, and published it in Union Street, now known as State Street. Up to April 6th, 1734, he signed his name as LOUIS TIMOTHEE; from that period he anglicized it to LEWIS TIMOTHY. His demise, the result of an "unhappy accident," took place in December, 1738.

In the issue of the *Gazette* of 21st June, 1735, the first wood-cut appeared—that of a horse; it bore but little resemblance to the object which it pretended to represent. The proprietor of the paper used it in an advertisement, inserted by FRAN. LE BRASSEUR, who made known the fact that "a bay mare had been taken astray on his plan- "tation, near Goose Creek."

The same paper, in its number of the 22nd January, 1737, mentions that " We have had so cold weather here,

" that in one night between Tuesday and Wednesday the
" water in the creeks and ponds in and about the Town,
" was frozen near three inches thick."

Having given data for cold weather, which can scarcely
be surpassed in Charleston, in point of severity, we have
concluded to quote from two authorities, in relation to the
intensity of the heat known here.

It is not unfrequently the case, that after having laid
aside the newspaper which has announced the " Hottest
Day," the reader is very apt to encounter in the daily intercourse with his fellow-citizens, some one of that class of
croakers, who having no moderation in their minds, give
evidence of the same deficiency in their conversation.
With them a moderate degree of language is seldom or
never given utterance to ; but on the other hand, the super-
lative degree is ever predominant. After the perusal of the
following extracts, the *quid nunc* will be convinced that
he has not as yet experienced the " Hottest Day" ever
known.

The Rev'd. Mr. HEWETT records a very remarkable
season of hot and dry weather. He says : " During the
" summer of 1728, the weather in Carolina was observed
" to be uncommonly hot, by which the face of the earth
" was entirely parched ; the pools of standing water dried
" up, and the beasts of the field reduced to the greatest
" distress."

Dr. CHALMERS speaks of the year 1752 as " excessively
" hot and dry in Charlestown ; many cattle perished for
" want of water ; the plants were shrunk and withered,
" and the distress of man and beast was indescribable.
" When the mercury rose to the 97 and 98 degrees of the
" thermometer in the shade, the atmosphere seemed in a
" glow. At bed time it was not possible to lie long still ;
" some of the inhabitants were compelled to lay about on

" the pavements. This circumstance is corroborated by
" the venerable JOSIAH SMITH, who informed me that so
" intense was the heat, that along the Bay he observed
" many families who had their beds made in their bal-
" conies."

" Bodies that died putrified in five hours, and a candle
" that was blown out at this season, and set in a chimney
" at 10 o'clock at night, the wick continued to burn clearly
" until next morning, and was likely to do so for many
" hours longer."

The following description of the first, and perhaps the
most serious fire which befell " Charlestown," is extracted
from *The South Carolina Gazette*, of the 20th November,
1740 :

On Tuesday, the 18th instant, a " Fire broke out in this
" Town, at 2 o'clock, on the afternoon, which consumed the
" houses from Broad Street and Church Street, down to
" Granville Bastion, (which was the most valuable part of
" the Town, on account of the buildings and trade), not-
" withstanding the utmost care and diligence of the inhab-
" itants of all ranks, who were very active in their endea-
" vors to extinguish it. The fire likewise consumed all the
" houses on the West side of Church Street from Broad
" Street, opposite to Col. BREWTONS,* which was saved with
" the greatest diligence, by blowing up several houses,
" which put a stop to the fire about 8 o'clock, at night.
" The wind blowing pretty fresh at North West, carried
" the flakes of fire so far, and by that means set houses on
" fire at such a distance, that it was not possible to prevent
" the spreading of it. On this unfortunate occurrence the

---

* Fraser in his " Reminiscences of Charlestown," published in 1854, de-
signated Col. Brewton's as the " old brick house on the West side of Church
Street, two doors South of the corner of Tradd Street." The Provincial Assembly had been, formerly, accommodated there by Col. Miles Brewton,
whose residence it was at that time.

" assistance given by the Commanders of His Majesty's
" ships was very considerable, in pulling down and blow-
" ing up houses, and particularly by extinguishing the fire
" in Granville's Bastion,* where part of the platform was
" consumed, and some of the gun carriages. The militia
" was ordered under arms, and proper guards placed in
" several parts of the Town, to prevent the embezzling of
" any of the sufferers' goods,† which were saved from the
" flames. There was a detachment from each of His Ma-
" jesty's ships *Phœnix*, *Tartar* and *Spence* on shore ; and a
" party of twenty troopers patrolled all night up to the
" Quarter House, and around the Town."

The next edition of this paper, which appeared the week
following, from November 27th to December 4th, 1740, was
almost entirely taken up with notices of removals and articles lost the night of the fire, one of the latter description
is here appended :

" WILLIAM WRIGHT, gold and silver-smith, is removed
" to John's Island, and continues to carry on his business,
" where gentlemen can be supplied with all sorts of work as
" usual ; his case will shortly be furnished with sundries,
" and kept by Mr. ELEAZER PHILLIPS, post master, on
" Madam TROTT's Wharff. The said WRIGHT, lost at the
" fire, out of his pocket, a long piece of gold, near a foot in
" length, and the breadth of a gold button. Whoever
" shall find the same, and bring it to ELEAZER PHILLIPS,

---

* Granville Bastion was where the last building on the East side of East
Bay now is.

† The copy of a letter written just after the fire by Robert Pringle, Judge
of the Court of Common Pleas, which his descendant, Judge W. Alston
Pringle has kindly permitted the author to see, states that " the loss in merchandize of all description was computed at two hundred thousand pounds
sterling. Two-thirds of the Town," this letter adds, " was destroyed in four
hours of time ; besides a great number of stores, there were consumed 300
dwelling houses, and had the fire occurred at night, at the same hour it did
in the day, a great number of lives might have been lost, and most of the
shipping might have likewise been destroyed."

"shall have three pounds reward, paid by said WRIGHT or " PHILLIPS."

This announcement from the post master, also appeared : " This is to give notice that the post office is now kept at "the house where Mr. PRIOLEAU'S scales are, on Madam " TROTT'S Wharff, by ELEAZER PHILLIPS."

The account of the fire of 1740, is by no means uninteresting. It cannot either be regarded as foreign to the subject matter, as it is from newspapers, the medium of news and correspondence, that the information has been gathered. It has occurred to the author, that continuing to mention, in their appropriate places, the principal fires which have happened in Charleston, will prove interesting and instructive. He is the more readily induced to this belief from the fact that, neglected as our State history has been, that of our City—which was for a length of time her capital, and chief resort, and is still her commercial metropolis—has received even less attention.

ELIZABETH, the widow of LEWIS TIMOTHY, carried on the *Gazette.* In the issue of the paper which followed the death of her husband, she makes this appeal to the patrons and the public, over her signature : " I take this "opportunity of informing the publick, that I shall con- "tinue the paper as usual ; and hope, by the assistance "of my friends, to make it as entertaining and correct as " may reasonably be expected. Wherefore, I flatter myself, " that all those persons, who by subscription, or otherwise, "assisted my late husband in the prosecution of the said "undertaking, will be kindly pleased to continue their fa- " vors and good offices to his poor afflicted widow, and six " small children, and another hourly expected."

She was succeeded, in 1757, by her son, PETER TIMO- THY, and his name, as publisher, appeared under the title of his paper. It was the first instance known in newspaper publication. Previously, the publisher's name was always placed at the bottom of the fourth page.

In connection with his younger brother, CHARLES, PETER continued to publish the paper " on the Bay, opposite the upper market ;" (now Vendue Range) afterwards, at the corner of King and Tradd Streets, under the firm of TIMOTHY & Bro., which lasted until the fall of " Charlestown," in May, 1780. Under their proprietorship, the paper was called the *Gazette of the State of South Carolina*. PETER TIMOTHY was taken prisoner by the British, after the fall of " Charlestown."

In *The South Carolina Gazette* of the 30th March, 1746, there appeared the appended presentment of the Grand Jury of the Province, made at " a Court of General Sessions of " the Peace, Oyer and Terminer, Assign and General Goal " Delivery." It began and was " holden at Charlestown, the " 18th day of March, Anno Domini 1746, before the Hon- "orable THOMAS DALE, WILLIAM BULL, jr., and JOHN " LINING, Esquires, Assistant Judges of our Lord the " King, as a grievance, did present Printer TIMOTHY, prin- "ter of the paper called the *South Carolina Gazette*, for "having printed and published, in the aforesaid *Gazette*, " No. 666, a letter signed R. A., and in No. 669, another "letter signed S. T., containing matter of falsehood, and " also libellous, and a great scandal and reflection upon His " Excellency (JAMES GLEN,) the Governor of this Pro- "vince, and tends to bring his authority into contempt ; " and, therefore, we request the Honorable Court to give " proper directions for punishing the author, printer and " publisher of the said two letters ; which we apprehend to " be destructive to the liberty of the press, a privilege we "enjoy, and which has been so justly contended for, by our "ancestors, and we hope will be preserved to our latest "posterity." The presentment of this Jury, over which

GABRIEL MANIGAULT, Esquire, was Foreman, is worthy of the space here accorded to it.

The article in No. 666, signed "R. A.," and referred to by this presentment as a grievance, was a protest by the writer, to the pious proposal of Governor GLEN to prevent, as much as possible, the profanation of the Lord's Day, by stopping the sale of "merchandize, meáts, fish and herbage."

"T. S.," the author of the other article in No. 669, presented by the jury, objected to, and disputed the right of His Excellency's placing sentinels at the Town gates every Sunday, to prevent the violation of the Sabbath, and prohibit idle persons from going "a pleasuring" on that day.

CHAPTER III.

IN December, 1765, *The South Carolina Gazette and
Country Journal* was published in Bedon's Alley, by
CHARLES CROUCH, a sound whig. He published it until
1772 ; then it was continued by his widow, MARY CROUCH,
until 1775.

CHARLES CROUCH, the publisher of *The South Carolina
Gazette and Country Journal*, was an apprentice to PETER
TIMOTHY. He died, 1772, leaving two sons, W. H. and
ABRAHAM CROUCH. CHARLES CROUCH, the publisher, was
the paternal grandfather of Mr. CHARLES W. CROUCH, an
old resident of this City. The title of the paper was chang-
ed, subsequently, to *South Carolina and American General
Gazette*, and published by ROBERT WELLS, at the "Old
Printing House." ROBERT WELLS was a staunch royalist.
ROBERT WELLS & SON were, afterwards, publishers of this
paper, at No. 71 Tradd Street. Its motto was from HOR-

ACE, " *Nullius adictus jurare in verba magistri.*" This
firm, " Printers to the King's Most Excellent Majesty,"
published the *Royal Gazette,* from March 3d, 1781, to the
close of 1782. Both father and son became, at a succeeding time, publishers of the *Nassau (New Providence)
Gazette.*

CROUCH'S *Country Journal,* in its number of the 29th
October, 1767, says: " At a full meeting of the Board of
" Commissioners for building the new ' Exchange and Cus-
" tom House,'* the proposals of Messrs. PETER and JOHN
" HORLBECK, were preferred ; and at the same time agreed
" with for finishing the same, by beginning of the year
" 1770, for forty thousand nine hundred and sixty-six
" pounds (currency equal to 5,848 sterling, or about $26,-
" 000), and the new Watch-house, already began, by the
" 1st of August next, by Messrs. NAILER & BROWN, for
" 5,500 currency ; also the stone bridge, at the North end
" of the Bay, for $3,300 currency."

From CROUCH'S *Country Journal,* of January, 1778, is
taken this account of the second disastrous fire in " Charlestown :"

" On Thursday, 15th instant, a little after 4 o'clock in
" the morning, a fire was discovered in the bake-house of
" one MOORE, at the North end of Union Street. The
" alarm being immediately given, a number of people, with
" engines, etc., assembled, but the wind blowing fresh at

---

* James R. Pringle, then Collector of the Port, by appointment of President Monroe, in 1819, in compliance with the wishes of the merchants of
Charleston, effected an arrangement with the Government, on the 9th November, 1833, by which the appropriate and serviceable cupola was, in the
winter of 1835, added to the Exchange building. Mr. Charles Fraser, the
artist, designed this cupola. J. H. Seyle and Albert Elfe were the builders.
The Exchange and Custom House was vacated on the 2d of June, 1843,
for necessary repairs, and the fixtures removed to Faber's building, corner
of East Bay and Fraser's Wharf. The repairs were completed, and the
building re-occupied 21st September, 1843.

"N.E., drove the flames with an impetuosity that could not
" be checked.   The fire was so rapid in its progress, that
" before twelve o'clock, it had entirely destroyed all Union
" Street, the South side of Queen Street from Mrs. DOY-
" LEY's house to the Bay, greatest part of Chalmer's Alley,
" all the Bay, excepting fifteen houses from Queen Street
" to Granville's Bastion ; the North side of Broad Street
" from Mr. THOMAS SMITH's house to the Bay ; the South
" side of the same from Mr. SAWAGEN's to Mr. GUERARD's ;
" all Gadsden's Alley, Elliott Street, excepting two houses ;
" Bedon's Alley ; the East side of Church Street from
" Broad Street to Stoll's Alley, excepting five tenements,
" and the whole of Tradd Street to the Eastward of Church
" Street.   The crackling of the flames, the dreadful columns
" of smoke, bearing with them myriad of fiery flakes,
" which fell in all parts of the Town, lying in the direction
" of the wind ; the roar of explosions ; the crash of falling
" houses ; the shrieks of the unhappy sufferers ; the horror
" painted in every countenance ; the confusion apparent
" everywhere, and detecting the infamous wretches (and
" they were not a few), who availed themselves of the op-
" portunity to pilfer, altogether formed one of the most
" dismal scenes of woe and distress that can possibly be
" conceived.   Much praise is due to the officers and soldiers
" quartered in Town, who afforded every assistance in their
" power to the inhabitants, and it was chiefly owing to
" their extraordinary exertions, that the houses at the
" South end of the Bay were preserved.   The fire did not
" proceed any further after twelve o'clock on the 15th, but
" it is not yet entirely extinguished.   The number of
" dwelling houses destroyed, exclusive of stores and out-
" houses is upwards of 250.   The quantity of merchandize
" and furniture is very considerable.   The whole loss by
" the most moderate computation exceeds three millions of

"dollars. Many are of the opinion it exceeds a million
"sterling. The number of lives lost, is not great. We
"have not heard of more than six, some of whom were
"negroes. The Charlestown Library Society's* valua-
"ble collection of books, instruments, and apparatus for
"astronomical and philosophical observations and experi-
"ments, etc., being unfortunately placed in a house, in the
"neighborhood of that in which the fire broke out, is almost
"entirely lost."†

Public notice was given on the evening of the 15th to
all those that were at a loss for lodgings and victuals, that
both were provided for them at the public expense, in the
several public buildings; and on the 16th, the General
Assembly voted £20,000 for the immediate relief of the
sufferers. The State of Georgia was not unmindful of suf-

---

*Shecut refers to this Library in his "Medical and Philosophical Essays."
"It was founded," he says, "by seventeen gentlemen, and that they obtained an Act of Incorporation in the year 1754." He adds, "the Library was
destroyed 17th January, 1778."

†The Journal under date of 5th February, says: "We have been informed
that the fire on the 15th of January, broke out in a kitchen, hired out to
some negroes, and not in Moore's bake-house. We were mistaken in say-
ing the fire did not spread any farther after 12 o'clock, on the 15th, as Major
Beckman's house, which was the last that took fire, was not in flames until
4 o'clock in the afternoon."

Elkanah Watson, in his Memoirs, abridged and published by his son, W.
C. Watson, in 1856, in a volume entitled "Men and Times of the Revolution,"
chapter iv, pages 44–45, makes mention of this conflagration. "I had passed
the evening of the 15th January, '78," he says, "with a brilliant party, at the
splendid mansion of a wealthy merchant of the City. In two hours after
we had left the scene of elegant refinement, the stately edifice, the rich
furniture, and all its gorgeous appliances, were wrapped in flames. In the
mid hours of a cold and tempestuous night, I was aroused by the cry of fire,
and by a loud knocking at the door, with the appalling intelligence—The
Town is in flames. I pressed forward to the theatre of one of the most
terrific conflagrations that ever visited Charlestown. The devastation was
frightful. The fire raged with unmitigated fury for seventeen hours.
Every vessel, shallop, and negro boat was crowded with the distressed inhabitants. Many who, a few hours before, retired to their beds in affluence,
were now reduced, by the all-devouring element, to indigence.

fering "Charlestown." Their Assembly generously voted $10,000 to relieve the distressed.

In March, 1783, *The South Carolina Gazette and General Advertiser* began an irregular publication, then semi-weekly, at 94 Church Street. It was conducted by JOHN MILLER, a public Printer, who came from London, England. He, in his proemial, alluded to his arrival in Philadelphia from the "Mother Country," in January, 1783, just after the news of the evacuation of "Charlestown" had been received there. That evacuation took place on the 14th of December, 1782, now eighty-eight years ago. Mr. MILLER made mention of the fact of his having been sent to "Charlestown" by the Honorable Delegation in Congress, to be Printer to the State. Our delegation, at that time, consisted of EDWARD RUTLEDGE, THOMAS HEYWARD, THOMAS LYNCH and ARTHUR MIDDLETON. Mr. MILLER closed his prefatory address to the people, among whom he came, thus : " My ambition could not have been " more truly gratified than finding myself the Printer of " the Commonwealth of South Carolina." His paper was,

---

" After laboring at the fire for many hours, I returned to my quarters, to obtain a brief respite. I had scarcely seated myself, before a man rushed in, exclaiming—' Your roof is on fire !' The mass of the conflagration was afar off, but it, as it were, rained fire. When we had extinguished the fire on the roof, I thought it time to remove my trunk, containing funds to a large amount. Not being able to obtain assistance, I was constrained to shoulder it myself. Staggering under my load, (a burden which in ordinary times I could scarcely have lifted,) I proceeded along Main Street. The fire had extended far and wide, and was bearing down in awful majesty, a sea of flame. Almost the whole of the spacious street exhibited on one side, a continuous and glaring blaze. My heart sickened at beholding half-dressed matrons, delicate young ladies, and children, wandering about unprotected, and in despair."

Elkanah Watson, in continuing his account of the fire, speaks of his having been prostrated on the ground alongside of his trunk, by the blowing up of a large building. His description of his hastening on, until he reached an elegant house (Governor Rutledge's), in the suburbs of the City, and there depositing his trunk, and his final recovery of it, is rather amusing.

3

at that time, printed on the East side of Church Street, within a few doors of Broad Street.

In *The South Carolina Gazette and General Advertiser*, of April 26th, 1783, Mr. MILLER, the proprietor, wrote in this wise of the restoration to peace : " Tuesday last was " a day ever to be remembered, such an one this State " never before enjoyed ; 'twas a period of its severe distress, " a confirmation of its Independence.   The pleasing coun- " tenances of its citizens on Monday, were truly expressive " of the pleasure they derived from receiving the official " account (published in the *Gazette* on Sunday) of the " conclusion of a war, begun on one side in injustice, car- " ried on in wickedness and folly ; and opposed on the " other from the strictest principle of self-defence, the " maintenance of their freedom and property."

In the *Gazette* of the 29th of April, 1783, THOMAS HALL, Clerk of the Court, Sheriff, etc., announced that he had just been appointed Post Master, and that he had " opened his office," at the State House, from " whence he " will send a rider northwardly, as far as Falmouth, in " Calco Bay, every Tuesday, at 6 o'clock, P. M.   Also, " one for Savannah, every Monday, at 10 o'clock, A. M. ; " thence he is to return, and meet the northern post on " Saturday."

At a later date, appeared this announcement from the Post Master : " Post Office, Charleston, Oct. 17, 1783. " The Post Master, desirous of extending the utility of " his office in a general manner, at the request of many " of the citizens, will, in future, receive letters for Eu- " rope, or any other part of the world, to be forwarded " by the first safe and convenient opportunity ; to defray " the charge of bags, etc., for the preservation of the " letters, the small and customary sum of one penny, with " each letter will be requisite.   Monday and Tuesday of

" each week, are the proper days for sending letters to the " post office, to go by land."

As ISAIAH THOMAS has told us that ELEAZER PHILLIPS was the " first Printer to His Majesty," it may, therefore, be safely stated—strengthened by the preceding notice, that after the night of the fire of the 18th of November, 1740, PHILLIPS had removed from Church Street to Madam TROTT's Wharff—that he was the first Post Master.

We will here trace the appointments of post masters to the present incumbent.

PHILLIPS was succeeded by GEORGE ROUPELL, who had the office in Tradd Street. ROUPELL was succeeded by PETER BOUNETHEAU, who received his commission from BENJAMIN FRANKLIN, then Post Master General of the United Colonies. His warrant* is dated 10th of May, 1777. THOMAS HALL, BOUNETHEAU's successor, whom the *Gazette* of the 29th April, 1783, announced had just been appointed Post Master, was succeeded by THOMAS W. BACOT, who at the close of the year 1791, was appointed by TIMOTHY PICKERING, then Post Master General, under the Administration of President GEORGE WASHINGTON. The 22nd of April, 1812, Mr. BACOT moved the office from 52 Tradd Street to 84 Broad Street, north side, a few doors west of the Court House. It was opened there the following day. " By direction of the Post Master General," the same authority says, " it was removed in May, 1815, to the Exchange building."†

Our highly esteemed and valued fellow-citizen, Honorable

---

* This warrant of Peter Bounetheau is now in the possession of his son, H. B. Bounetheau, of Charleston.

† That structure, the present "old post office," was then an open arched vestibule. The building was the property of the City. It was, subsequently, bartered to the United States government, the City taking in exchange the present "City Hall," and giving a bonus of $2,000 to the government for the purpose of fitting up the post office.

ALFRED HUGER, was in turn appointed Post Master, by President ANDREW JACKSON, and he entered upon the duties of his office on the 1st of January, 1835. After the capture of the City, by the United States forces—18th of February, 1865—Mr. A. M. MARKLAND, a special Agent of the Government, took charge on the 22nd, and acted as Post Master, at the South West corner of King and George Streets; this was pending the arrival of STANLEY G. TROTT. Mr. TROTT became, by appointment, in April, 1867, the seventh Post Master this City has known, and the third since the adoption of the Constitution. This latter appointment has given entire satisfaction.

CHAPTER IV.

CHARLESTON INCORPORATED—THIRTEEN WARDS CREA-
TED—FIRST WARDENS—REPRESENTATIVES OF THE PAR-
ISHES OF ST. PHILIP AND ST. MICHAEL—FIRST INTEND-
ANT—ELECTIONS ENDORSED BY THE PRESS—THE BELLS
OF ST. MICHAEL'S CHURCH—THE FIRST CIRCULATING LI-
BRARY, 1783—JOHN MILLER—HIS WEEKLY MESSEN-
GER—DEATH OF JOHN MILLER—COLUMBIAN HERALD OR
THE PATRIOTIC COURIER OF NORTH AMERICA—OTHER
PAPERS AND THEIR EDITORS—THIRD AND FOURTH DIS-
ASTROUS FIRES, 1796 AND 1800.

ON the 13th of August, 1783, there was published in
the *Gazette* the act incorporating Charleston. The seal of
the City was adopted by the proprietor of the paper as a
vignette. The obverse was at the head of the paper on
one side, while the reverse was placed on the other. The
title of the journal, set as it was in three different de-
scriptions of type, old style double pica, pica capitals and
double small pica italics, occupied the space between the
obverse and reverse of the seal. The Act of Incorporation, provided that " Charlestown" should hereafter be
called and known by the name of " the City of Charleston," and should be divided into the following Wards : *

---

*The City is now divided into eight wards, and sixteen precincts. The
intersection of Meeting and Queen Streets, forming the internal boundary
of the lower four ones, and what may appear a little curious, if a person
were to stand on the central point of said intersection, he might be said to
have a footing on all of the four, or lower wards, at once.

"No. 1. From Wilkin's Fort, East side of Church "Street, to the South side of Tradd Street, easterly to the "Bay.

"No. 2. From the North side of Tradd Street, to the "South side of Queen Street, easterly.

"No. 3. From the North side of Queen Street, to the "South side of Ellery Street, (now Pinckney) easterly.

"No. 4. From the North side of Ellery Street, up to "Meeting Street, and along the same to the West end of "Queen Street, through Anson Street to Boundary (now "Calhoun) Street, easterly.

"No. 5. From the South end of King Street, to the "South side of Tradd Street, easterly, to Church Street.

"No. 6. From Tradd Street, along King Street, to the "South side of Broad Street, easterly.

"No. 7. From North side of Broad Street, along King "Street, to the South side of Queen Street, easterly, to "Church Street.

"No. 8. From the North side of Queen Street, along "King Street, South of Hazell Street, easterly, to join the "Ward No. 3.

"No. 9. From Hazell Street, along King Street, to "Boundary Street, and to join the Ward No. 4, easterly.

"No. 10. From the South end of Legaré Street, includ-"ing the West end of Tradd Street, easterly, to King "Street.

"No. 11. From the North side of Tradd Street, to the "West end of Broad Street, easterly, to King Street.

"No. 12. From the North side of Broad Street, to the "West end of Ellery Street, easterly, to King Street.

"No. 13. From the North side of Ellery Street, West to "Boundary Street, easterly, to King Street.

"And it is further enacted by the authority aforesaid, "That the Church Wardens of the Parishes of St. Philip

" and St. Michael shall within one month after passing this
" act, give ten days public notice that Wardens are to be
" chosen for each Ward, whose qualifications shall be the
" same as that for a member of the House of Representa-
" tives; and that all free white persons residing in each
" Ward, being citizens of this State, who were taxed three
" shillings sterling, the preceding year, or are taxed three
" shillings sterling in the present year, towards the support
" of the government of this State, shall be entitled to vote
" for a Warden for their respective Ward; and they shall
" also notify the time and place, when and where, the elec-
" tion is to be held in each Ward, and appoint proper per-
" sons for managing and conducting the same; and the
" said persons after the election is ended, shall make a
" return to the Church Wardens of the persons chosen
" Wardens of the respective Wards; and the said Church
" Wardens shall give notice to the several persons of their
" appointment respectively, and summon them to meet
" together at any time and place, within ten days after
" their election, for the purpose of taking the oath of qual-
" ification, allegiance, and office, prescribed by the law,
" which oath may be administered by any one Warden to
" the other. Provided, seven shall be present at the time
" of administering of the same.

" In pursuance of the above act, we, the subscribers,
" Church Wardens of the Parishes of Saint Philip and
" Saint Michael, give this public notice, that Monday, the
" first day of September next, is fixed for the holding of
" the said election, from ten to twelve o'clock in the fore-
" noon, and from two to four in the afternoon; and the
" following gentlemen are hereby appointed to superintend
" the same, viz. :

" Ward No. 1. JOHN COX, No. 46, corner of Lynch's
" Lane.

"Ward No. 2. Samuel Legaré, No. 26½ Church Street.

"Ward No. 3. Sims White, at St. Philip's Church.

"Ward No. 4. Colonel Lushington, at No. 3 Hazell "Street.

"Ward No. 5. Edward Lightwood, at the Scotch Pres-"byterian Church.

"Ward No. 6. Benjamin Villepontoux, at his house, "No. 77, corner of Tradd and King Streets.

"Ward No 7. Thomas Eveleigh, at No. 3, behind the "State House.

"Ward No. 8. Hugh Swinton, at his house, No.—, in "Meeting Street.

"Ward No. 9. Thomas Radcliffe, jr., at his house, No. "1 George Street.

"Ward No. 10. Isaac Holmes, No. 8 Legaré Street.

"Ward No. 11. William Price, at his house, No. 39 "Tradd Street.

"Ward No. 12. Dr. Tucker Harris, at his house, No. "147 King Street.

"Ward No. 13. Robert Ladson, at his house, No. 4 "Wentworth Street.

"At which places of election all persons duly entitled to "vote in their respective Wards are desired to attend.

"James Bentham,

"Lambert Lance,

"*Church Wardens for St. Philip.*

"Daniel Hall,

"Phillip Prioleau.

"*Church Wardens for St. Michael.*

"Charleston, August 18, 1783."

On the morning of Tuesday, the 2nd of September, 1783, the result of the election for members to represent the Parishes of St. Philip and St. Michael, in the General Assembly, and for Wardens, is given.

" Yesterday, came on the election for three members to
" represent the Parishes of St. Philip and St. Michael,
" when at the close of the ballots this day, the following
" gentlemen were declared duly elected :

" Hon. W. H. GIBBES, Hon. J. F. GRIMKE, and THOMAS
SHUBRICK.

" Yesterday, came on in the different Wards, the election
" for Wardens of this City, when the following gentlemen
" were chosen :

" Ward No. 1, JAMES NEILSON ; Ward No. 2, THOMAS
" BEE ; Ward No. 3, A. ALEXANDER ; Ward No. 4, B.
" BEEKMAN ; Ward No. 5, JOSHUA WARD ; Ward No. 6,
" THOMAS HEYWARD ; Ward No. 7, JOHN MATHEWS ; Ward
" No. 8, GEORGE FLAGG ; Ward No. 9, THOMAS RADCLIFFE,
" jr. ; Ward No. 10, ISAAC HOLMES ; Ward No. 11, RICHARD
" HUTSON ; Ward No. 12, JOHN WARING ; Ward No. 13,"
no election.   The two candidates who stood highest in this
Ward had an equal number of votes.   To supply this va-
cancy consequent by a tie vote, another election was held
on the 2d October, following, when ROBERT LADSON received the largest number of votes.

In the *Gazette*, the second day after the general election,
it was announced that

" Pursuant to the Act of the General Assembly to incor-
" porate Charleston, the Wardens duly elected and qualified
" this day, agreeable to the directions of the said act,
" hereby give public notice, that Thursday, the 11th day
" of September, instant, is fixed upon for the election of an
" Intendant for the City, from among the Wardens ; and
" that all persons qualified to vote for Wardens in their
" respective Wards, will be entitled to vote for such In-
" tendant.   That the election will be held under the Ex-
" change of the said City, from the hours of nine to twelve
" in the forenoon, and from two to five in the afternoon,

" when and where the subscribers will attend to manage
" the same.

> " JAMES BENTHAM,
> " LAMBERT LANCE,
> " PHILLIP PRIOLEAU,
> " DANIEL HALL.

" Thursday, came on the election of Intendant for this
" City, agreeable to the Act of Incorporation, when RICH-
" ARD HUTSON, Esq., was chosen. After the election,
" Messrs. BENTHAM, LANCE, HALL and PRIOLEAU, the
" returning officers, waited on Mr. HUTSON, to acquaint
" him of the issue of the election, and although he had in
" the most pressing manner requested the citizens not to
" vote for him, it cannot be mentioned too much to his
" honor, that on finding the voice of his fellow-citizens
" had declared him their Intendant, he instantly gave up
" his own private wishes, and cheerfully accepted the bur-
" then they had laid upon him. After which, he went
" with the above gentlemen to Mr. MCCRADY'S, where an
" elegant entertainment was provided, and where the citi-
" zens, on this novel and pleasing occasion, had the happi-
" ness to congratulate the Intendant on his election."

The editor of the *Gazette*, in alluding to the election,
remarked, that " a private station is not the post of honor ;
" yet, in the present instance, happy may those gentlemen
" be said to be, on whom the election did not fall. In the
" first year of Incorporation, the office of Intendant will
" prove a most arduous and laborious task. Though it has
" been forced on Mr. HUTSON, yet the public are satisfied
" they shall not be disappointed of his every exertion to
" contribute to their peace and happiness by the full exer-
" cise of his great abilities, and integrity in accomplishing
" the great objects of *regulation and reform*, pointed out
" by the Incorporation Act."

" This is a new era in the history of Charleston ; may it
" be propitious to its rising glory, increasing commerce,
" and growing opulence; and on this occasion we could
" wish to do away a prejudice (and nothing but which can
" prevent its becoming the first City in America,) enter-
" tained in Europe against Charleston, on misinformation
" of its being unhealthy. The printer thinks he owes it to
" truth to declare, that so far from finding the climate of
" South Carolina, as they conceive, unfavorable to any Euro-
" pean constitution, he has not had an hour's illness since his
" arrival in this State, nor does he remember to have
" enjoyed, for the same length of time, such an uninter-
" rupted state of health. From the best information, we
" may venture to say, there is not a more healthy City on
" the continent."

Intendant HUTSON served until the 14th of the following September. He was then succeeded by Col. ARNOL-
DUS VANDERHORST.

On Saturday morning, 22d November, 1783, Mr. MIL-
LER published, in this quaint and ambiguous style, the
subjoined information :

" THURSDAY MORNING, 10 o'CLOCK.
. " The public will believe Mr. MILLER has no little
" happiness in informing them, that the *Lightning* may
" shortly be expected. Off Edisto, the second mate came
" on shore, from whom a gentleman learnt, who is just
" arrived in Town, that she brings Mr. M. almost as many
" children as she brings them bells. She is about three
" leagues to the southward."

These bells which Mr. MILLER alluded to, have a memorable record. They are St. Michael's chime, eight in
number, and were purchased in England, in 1764. The
ship *Little Carpenter* brought them to " Charlestown,"
July 17, 1764. Major TRAILLE, of the Royal Artillery,

took them away at the evacuation of December, 1782. They were sent back to "Charlestown" in the *Lightning*, and arrived here 20th November, 1783. During the last war, they were sent to Columbia, and were destroyed at the sack and destruction of that City, in February, 1864. The fragments were sent to England in the spring of 1866, and re-cast, a century after, by decendants of the original manufacturers. They were landed in Charleston from the Norwegian bark *Gladstone*, February 18, 1867, and were again rung March 21, 1867.

About the close of the year 1783, Mr. MILLER established, with the aid of several prominent gentlemen, a Public or Circulating Library. "This was," as he said, "with a view of supplying the present scarcity of books, "arising from the devastation made in gentlemen's private "libraries, in the Gothic, savage and wanton wish of the "British Army, to exterminate all knowledge."

JOHN MILLER sold *The Gazette and Advertiser* to TIMOTHY & MASON, and went to Pendleton, in this State. There he published *Miller's Weekly Messenger*. This journal changed hands, and was known for many years as the *Pendleton Messenger*.* The editor and publisher, JOHN MILLER, died in Pendleton, in 1809, and was buried at the "Old Stone Church."

Between 1783, the year in which the act incorporating Charleston was passed, and 1795, a period of twelve years, there were but two diurnal publications in this City. One was *The Columbian Herald or Patriotic Courier of North America*, published by Messrs. HARRISON and

---

* The rapid increase of the population of the upper portion of South Carolina must have been the inducement for Mr. Miller to go to Pendleton. Ramsay states, that in the two new western districts, now called Pendleton and Greenville, which were obtained by treaty founded on conquest from the Cherokee Indians, in 1771, filled so rapidly with inhabitants, that in the year 1800, they alone contained upwards of 30,000 souls.

BOWEN, then by THOMAS BARTHOLEMEW BOWEN and J. MARKLAND, as BOWEN and MARKLAND, at 4 Queen Street; afterwards (1784,) it was published at 15 Meeting Street; then, removed to No. 92 Church Street. This last removal took place on the 9th of May, 1795. The motto of this paper was, this constituent part of the Constitution of the State of South Carolina: "That the liberty of the press is inviolably preserved." *The Columbian Herald* had a bust of WASHINGTON as a vignette.

Mr. BOWEN had been a Lieutenant in the British Navy, possessed fine literary taste, and was once the publisher of *The South Carolina Weekly Messenger*. Prominent as a Mason, he was, anterior to 1800, a Grand Officer of the Grand Lodge of South Carolina.

The other paper was *The Charleston Evening Gazette*, printed by J. V. BURD and R. HASWELL, at 102 Broad Street. *The Evening Gazette* was, afterwards, printed by J. V. BURD, at 24 East Bay. JOSEPH VINCENT BURD died, after a short illness, on the 4th of October, 1785. He was, at the time, editor and proprietor of *The Georgetown Times*.

The City papers were, at that time, unsatisfactory as to their marine reports. The arrival and departure of vessels, and the names of their captains alone were mentioned. No distinction was made in the "making up" between that which was written and that which was selected. The type, too, was large, and inartistic.

Subsequent to 1783, there came into life *The Charleston Morning Post*, printed by CHILDS, HASWELL & McIVER. There was, also, *The City Gazette and Daily Advertiser*, printed by MARKLAND & McIVER, "Printers to the City," at 47 East Bay, from 1789 to 1797. This paper, of the 22nd of March, 1791, contained the Act to Incorporate

Camden, ratified 19th February, 1791. PETER FRENAU and SETH PAINE published it from 1797 to January, 1801. They were succeeded, January 1, 1801, by JOHN McIVER, who was at one time associated with Messrs. CHILDS & HASWELL, as before mentioned. Nothing is known farther than this of either CHILDS or HASWELL.

JOHN McIVER died May 7, 1801, in the neighborhood of this City, aged 37 years. It is a tribute fully due the memory of this gentleman to say, that to a cultivated understanding, he added a most benevolent disposition. At the time of his death he was a Senator in our State Legislature, from the united districts of Darlington, Marlboro and Chesterfield.

The most alarming fire, since that of 1778, occurred 13th June, 1796. It broke out in Lodge Alley,* on the afternoon of that day. " It baffled," says the account, " all ex-"ertions of a numerous concourse of citizens who speedily "assembled to extinguish the devouring flames, till Tues-"day morning, when a considerable part of the City was "laid in ashes. Every house in Queen Street, from the "Bay to the corner of Church Street; all Union Street "continued; two-thirds of Union Street; Church Street "from Broad Street to St. Philip's Church, with only two "exceptions; Chalmers and Berresford's Alley; Kinloch's "Court, and the North side of Broad Street from the State "House to Mr. JACK's, four doors below Church Street, "and five houses on the Bay, from the corner of Queen "Street, were burnt to the ground. The public buildings "destroyed are the French Church, and several adjoining "buildings. St. Philip's Church was on fire at different "times, and ultimately must have been destroyed, if a

---

* This Alley derived its name from the fact that all the Masonic Lodges once held their Communications in a building located in it.

"spirited negro man* had not ascended to the top of the
"cupola, next to the vane, and torn off the shingles. The
"private buildings destroyed, and the property they con-
"tained, are of immense amount. Five hundred chimneys
"have been counted, from which the buildings have been
"burnt; and £150,000 sterling is supposed to be a sum
"far short of the value of those buildings. The goods and
"furniture destroyed, are probably nearly equal to this
"sum."

B. F. PRITCHARD, an apprentice to W. P. YOUNG, Printer and Bookbinder, was blown up during the prevalence
of this fire.

The City Gazette and Daily Advertiser, in its issue of
Tuesday, 5th August, 1800, is the source from whence
is taken the account of another fire, four years after:
"Yesterday forenoon, between the hours of 10 and 11
"o'clock, a fire broke out, at the upper end, three doors
"above Boundary Street, on the West side, in the house of
"Mr. MARTIN MILLER, which destroyed five houses on
"that side of King Street; and before its progress could
"be arrested, eleven on the East side. The wind being

---

* Gospel Messenger, vol. xxiv, chapter xvii, page 168, 1796; August 14th—
The following letter of General C. Gadsden and Col. John Huger, was laid
before the Vestry :

"Gentlemen—Agreeably to your desire, united with a request from Major
Charles Lining to appraise a negro man at present his property, for the express purpose of his being liberated, and as a reward for his having extinguished the flames which in the late conflagration on the 13th ultimo had
been communicated to St. Philip's Church, but by his uncommon and particular exertion at the awful moment that venerable building was preserved;
and having seen the said Will, and being likewise well acquainted with his
character and profession, we have duly considered the subject referred to
us, both with respect to his qualifications and the price of negroes at this
juncture, and we have estimated and ascertained the value of the said Will,
at one hundred and seventy-five pounds."

"Agreed to, Mr. Lining giving £10."

"The fellow being called and informed of his emancipation, requested
that he may in future be called Will Philip Lining."

" at South West drove the flames from the City, otherwise,
" in all probability, the destitution would have been much
" greater than it is. The tobacco inspection, which was to
" leeward of the flames, caught twice, but by timely assist-
" ance the flame was extinguished. We understand the
" fire was occasioned by Mr. MILLER's attempting to stop
" a leak in a cask of brandy, in closing which a candle was
" held too near the liquor, which immediately caught, and
" in a few minutes communicated to some gunpowder, the
" explosion of which put the house in flames. We are
" sorry to add that Mr. and Mrs. MILLER were burned in
" a dreadful manner. The life of Mrs. MILLER was des-
" pared of last evening.

   " The principal sufferers by this calamity, are Mr. MIL-
" LER and Mrs. BRUNION, Mr. WILLIS, Mr. TURNER, Mr.
" VAUGHAN, Mr. PELOT, and Mrs. LEVIN, on the West
" side; and on the East side Mr. McMILLAN, who lost
" three houses, and his large range of stables. Mr. GREY,
" Mr. PRESSLEY, Mr. SIMMONS, Mr. CRAWFORD, Mrs. SIN-
" GLETON, Mr. McCRACKEN, and Messrs. WALSH & SONS.
" Mr. SAMUEL WELL's house was pulled down to prevent
" the fire from spreading. Notwithstanding the extreme
" heat of the day, the citizens repaired to the spot with
" the greatest alacrity, and afforded their assistance with a
" cheerfulness that has never been exceeded.

   " The consequences of the destructive fire of yesterday,
" are chiefly confined to that class of citizens whose all
" was exposed to the ravages of that destructive element.
" It is, therefore, to be hoped, that the most active and
" influential citizens, agreeably to their accustomed human-
" ity, will, on this afflicting occasion, come forward, and by
" their example and endeavors, take immediate measures
" for the relief of the unfortunate sufferers. It is, there-
" fore, respectfully suggested, that a meeting of the inhabi-

" tants to-morrow at 12 o'clock, at the Exchange, would be
" calculated to carry the object contemplated into imme-
" diate and complete effect."

Previous to June, 1783, we learn from the *Gazette*, fires
were extinguished by citizens who obtained water from the
City pumps, or drew it from wells by the tedious operation
of sinking buckets.   In June, 1784, a company was formed, called " Hand-in-Hand Fire Company."   The members
of this company were not only required to hand buckets of
water one to another, but were called upon to rescue from
the flames the private property of the individual members
of their association.   This institution had its use, but it was
far short of that philanthropic and general organization
into which the interested inhabitants of the City ought to
have formed themselves.   This " Hand-in-Hand Company," the first of these organizations here, and the nucleus
of our present efficient fire brigade, was governed by rules
of similar companies in New York and Philadelphia.
There seemed not to have been any regular formation of
engine companies, as now exist, before the year 1786.   The
following advertisement of RICHARD HUMPHREYS, jr., which
was publishd in the *Gazette* of January 24, 1786, confirms
the foregoing :

" The subscriber being informed that a number of gen-
" tlemen of this City, are about entering into that useful
" institution of fire companies, he will engage to supply
" them with any number of buckets they shall please to
" order."

CHAPTER V.

> Well did our papers here display the times;
> Some streak'd with follies; others, stain'd with crimes.

February 9, 1786.—A reward of four guineas is offered
by ANDREW PLEYM, through the paper of this date for the
perpetrator of a robbery at his store, between his dwelling
house, 106 Meeting Street, and the Smith's forge, at the
corner of Moor Street, (now Cumberland Street.)

February 13, 1786.—In this edition of the *Gazette*, is
the obituary of Mr. MATHEW BAYLEY, who died "some-
"time ago at Jones' Creek, a branch of Peedee, in North
"Carolina, aged 136; he was baptized when 134 years old."

"On the night of 16th February, 1786, at a quarter
"past 10 o'clock, as Mr. PHILIP MOSES, accompanied by
"his wife, was going home, two tall lusty men, dressed in
"short light colored clothes, stopped him in Broad Street,
"at the corner of Gadsden's Alley, in a manner that
"evinced the intention to rob him. Upon his making
"some resistance, one of the ruffians drew a pistol and

" fired at him, the explosion of which burned his face;
" the other fellow also fired, and both balls lodged in the
" adjacent house, fortunately without any mischief. AR-
" NOLDUS VANDERHORST, then Intendant, offered a reward
" of $200, on the morning of 27th February, for this
" attempt to rob and murder."

March 16, 1786.—" Two persons dressed in the Moorish
" habit are now in this City, and are supposed to be the
" same men that were taken into custody in Virginia, on
" suspicion of their being Algerines. The singularity of
" their dress induced a young gentleman of the law, to ask
" them some questions, which were answered with so much
" impertinence and vulgarity, that the gentleman proceed-
" ed to give one of the fellows a little manual correction,
" by way of reforming his manners. A mob immediately
" assembled, and the men were taken up; being carried
" to the home of a lady on the Bay, who understood their
" language, they appeared to be two men of the Jewish
" nation, who had landed in Virginia from Algiers, and
" had travelled over-land from that State to this."

May 22, 1786.—" JOHN GIBBONS advertised to be leased
" for seven years, to the highest bidder, on Tuesday, the 6th
" day of June next, that most agreeably situated farm at
" Haddrell's Point, commonly called Mt. Pleasant, con-
" taining about 80 acres, belonging to the estate of JACOB
" MOTT."

May 25, 1786.—" The commissioners appointed by the
" Legislature, for laying out the Town of Columbia, have
" appointed the first sale of lots to take place on the 2d
" September next, in this City." The records of the State
were removed from Charleston to Columbia, by direction of
the Legislature, in the winter of 1790.

September 21, 1786.—" We learn from London, that the
" re-publication of Dr. RAMSAY'S History of South Caro-

"lina, is deemed illegal in that country, on account of the
"long catalogue of British villanies and murders it con-
"tains."

The pages which contained the Declaration of Independence, DRAYTON'S charge against the King, etc., and many
strong accusations against Earl CORNWALLIS, Lord RAW-
DON, BROWN, MONCRIEF, TARLTON, TUCK, etc., were declared to be sufficient grounds for an expensive and vex-
atious prosecution from the crown lawyers, besides expos-
ing the publisher to personal violence, from the parties of
their zealous votaries.

June 19, 1796.—"On Thursday last, between ten and
"eleven o'clock in the forenoon, a fire broke out in a soap
"boiler's shop in Gadsden's Alley, which increased with
"the greatest rapidity for a considerable time, and seemed
"to threaten this City with a general conflagration. Fifteen
"capital houses, exclusive of a number of back buildings,
"were reduced to ashes. The loss in houses and other prop-
"erty is very great, for the fire was so versatile, that goods
"supposed to be in the greatest security, were obliged to be
"removed about, at different times, in the utmost haste, con-
"sequently they were much damaged; and several persons
"taking advantage of the confusion, secreted great quanti-
"ties; some that were detected have been committed to
"prison. Some supposing themselves secure, did not move
"at all, and lost every thing. Mr. BLAKELEY'S situation,
"at this time, was truly unfortunate as distressing, having,
"only the day before, finished moving the whole of his prop-
"erty, the chief of which, owing to his apparent security,
"and shifting of the wind, was destroyed. Mr. JAMES
"STRICKLAND, in conducting a cart heavily loaded, fell out
"of it, and the wheels went over his breast, which occasion-
"ed his death in the course of a few hours. Several per-
"sons were also much bruised and wounded."

The following is a list of persons who were burnt out, as given by the *Gazette*, viz. :

Messrs. WILLIAM SMITH & Co., Messrs. WELLS and BETHUNE, Mr. M'CREDIE, Mr. GERSHON COHEN, Messrs. M'AULEY and DAVIS, Messrs. ROBERT and HALL STEWART, Mr. JOHN AITKIN, Messrs. MUIRHEAD and MUNRO, and Mr. ABERNETHIE, THOMAS SMITH, Mr. SAMUEL BLAKELEY, Mr. HENRY MAIN STROMER—Mrs. GAULTIER, WILLIAM LOGAN, Dr. ROBERT WILSON.

On the morning of 22d June, 1786, the *Gazette* was published as a half-sheet. The publisher, while apologizing for it, stated that it was in consequence of the death of a grand-son, Master PETER WESTON. This number of the paper also contained a special notice from the proprietor, to this end : " To prevent a misunderstanding, adver-"tisements not exceeding twelve lines are inserted for three " shillings the first publication, and two shillings each con-"tinuation."

Most prominent in the criminal record at that time, was the murder of Mr. NICHOLAS JOHN WIGHTMAN, in his 25th year. The reader can see, while passing the western grave yard of St. Philip's Church, the slab which marks the spot where this gentleman was buried. The inscription states that " Divine Providence ordained it " so, that a single button belonging to the coat of the mur-" derer served, with other proof, to discover and convict "him." The account of the deed is given in the *Gazette*, March 17, 1788, in connection with a highway robbery which took place the same night. " Last Wednesday " night, between the hours of 10 and 11 o'clock, as Captain " MARSTON was returning on board his vessel, lying at " Mey's wharf, he was stopped near the Governor's bridge, " and robbed of his watch, some money, etc., by three vil-"lains, one of whom run a pistol full in his face, and

" would, in all probability, have taken his life, had not an
" accomplice prevented it; after which they left Captain
" MARSTON, and proceeded towards Meeting Street, where
" Mr. NICHOLAS JOHN WIGHTMAN was, soon after, shot
" through the heart, supposed by one of the same party.
" Information being sent to the guard-house, Captain DA-
" VIS, with proper assistance proceeded to the suspected
" spot where the murder was committed, at which place
" JOSIAH JORDAN, ROBERT STACEY, JOHN GEORGE, and
" others, were found, and taken into custody. One of them,
" EDWARD HATCHER, who being duly sworn, made oath
" and acknowledged, that last evening, near 11 o'clock,
" being the 12th day of March, 1788, he, in company with
" ROBERT STACEY, was standing at the door of THOMAS
" JONES, in Meeting Street, (between Market and Hayne
" Streets,) when a man walked past, and after he had gone
" about three doors farther, ROBERT STACEY followed,
" turned right before him, and with a brass barrel pistol
" shot him in the left breast, on which he fell and expired
" immediately. Said deponent believes that ROBERT STA-
" CEY designed to rob the deceased, but was prevented
" by people coming out with a light. HATCHER further
" states that JOSIAH JORDAN, JOHN GEORGE, ROBERT STA-
" CEY, THOMAS SMITH, ANDREW KEATING, ANN JONES,
" ANN CONNELLY, KATE CROWDY, and REBECCA STACEY,
" were, altogether, in said house, and that he saw ANN
" CONNELLY deliver out to the said STACEY, powder and
" ball—two balls and three swan shot—and directed him to
" go out and rob again, and, if he met with resistance, to
" fire on them."

In additional particulars, published on the 20th, the
Gazette returns thanks to Dr. LYNAH, the physician called
in, and Captain DAVIS, of the guard. STACEY, JORDAN,

GEORGE, SMITH, HATCHER, and ANN CONNELLY received sentence of death for the murder of Mr. WIGHTMAN.

A few evenings following Mr. WIGHTMAN'S murder, three villains went to the house of Mr. DANIEL MA-ZYCK, at Hampstead; but one of them, who had secreted himself under the house, receiving a violent blow with a sword, the knaves fled. The same evening, a gang of ruffians attacked a gentleman near Pinckney Street, but he escaped after receiving a slight wound with a cutlass, inflicted by one of the villains.

To the marriage of Mr. JAMES HIBBEN, and Miss SARAH WELLS, which appeared in the issue of January 28, 1788, there is appended these strange lines:

> " Farewell, my friend, but record
> The sufferings of your dying Lord!
> Let neither friends nor riches prove
> The total loss you bore for love."

On the morning of the 5th February, 1788, Mr. HIBBEN, over his signature, writes to the publisher:

" Please insert the following, in answer to some lines " which appeared in your *Gazette* of the 28th January, on " the morning of the subscriber's marriage, and oblige your " humble servant:

> " Welcome, my friend, you're free'd from schism,
> From canting, whining Methodism;
> You're now in a superior class,
> Ne'er heed the braying of an ass."

The above, as well as the succeeding selections, are made chiefly with the intent to show the style then adopted of promulgating sensational news; a style which seems less exceptionable to similar details of the present day, and withal fit for the public eye, and a place in a public journal.

" Branded, June 7, 1788, *John Cooper, William Irons,*
" *Thomas Jones, Richard Glascock, John Cunningham,*
" *John Shields, John Bruce,* and *Thomas Keely,* for lar-
" ceny."

" Hanged, June 11, 1788, pursuant to sentence, *Robert*
" *Stacey, Josiah Jordan, John George, Thomas Smith, Ed-*
" *ward Hatcher,* and *Ann Connelly,* for the murder of
" NICHOLAS JOHN WIGHTMAN."

" On 16th June, 1788, were executed, pursuant to sen-
" tence of the Court of Admiralty Sessions, for piracy, on
" the American Seas, *Captain William Rogers,* of New Lon-
" don, in Connecticut; *John Masters,* of Cheshire, in Eng-
" land, and *William Pendergrass,* of Derbyshire, in Eng-
" land, charged and found guilty of the murder of Mr.
" ABRAHAM NATHAN, of the Jewish nation, (joint owner
" with *Rogers,*) and passenger on board the sloop *Betsey,* in
" October last. Also, *Richard Williams* and *William Cain,*
" both of England, for the murder of Captain NATHANIEL
" C. WEBB, and Mr. CLODE or McCLODE, on the 18th or 20th
" May last, on board the schooner *Two Friends.* The un-
" happy *Rogers* appeared uncommonly penitent and resign-
" ed, from the day of his being apprehended, to the moment
" of his execution, when he solicited the attendance of the
" CLERGY, and joined in pathetic PRAYER to the SUPREME
" BEING, soliciting the pardon of his GOD for every trespass
" he had committed, and the forgiveness of every mortal
" that felt himself injured by him. He, to the last, denied
" having wilfully or maliciously killed Mr. NATHAN, and
" uniformly persisted in the declaration that he was not in
" sound mind when the bloody transaction took place; and
" that he was subject to fits of lunacy, which the cousin of
" Governor FANNING, and several others from that State,
" have likewise declared, as also to his being addicted to
" strong liquor, which always bereaved him of his reason.

5

" This assertion *Rogers* has repeatedly made to Mr. PHAE-
" LON, both before and after his trial, and to divers other
" gentlemen, as he likewise has, in sundry parts of a narra-
" tive of his life, which he had been writing several days
" prior to his death. The contemplation of having an aged
" father and mother, an affectionate, respectable wife and
" five young children, seemed to distress him beyond ex-
" pression or description, and deeply affect the numerous
" spectators, male and female. *Rogers*, repeatedly, at the
" spot of execution, begged the prayers of all present, and
" as often conjured Major PHAELON to give good advice
" and direction to his unfortunate babes."

TIMOTHY & MASON were publishers of the *Gazette* for
about three years, from January, 1797. Under them,
the paper was called *South Carolina State Gazette, and
Timothy and Mason's Daily Advertiser*. Its motto was :
" The public will be our guide—the public good our end."

In TIMOTHY & MASON'S *Gazette and Advertiser*, of 2d
January, 1797, we find among the advertisers, names
familiar to us at this time. Among those who advertised
vessels up for London, Liverpool, and other English and
American ports, were W. & E. CRAFTS, THOMAS MORRIS,
JOHN HASLETT & CO., ROBERT HAZELHURST & CO., HEN-
RY ELLISON, CORRIE & SCHEPELER, MURE & BOYD, CAMP-
BELL, HARVEY & CO., E. COFFIN, CROCKER, HICHBORN
& WRIGHT, NICHOLAS NORRIS, THOMAS TURNER, JOHN
TEASDALE, SAMUEL WATSON, J. & E. GARDNER & CO.
Those in the importing and grocery trade, were ANDREW
MCKENZIE, THOMAS HOOPER & CO., J. WINTHROP, WEBB
& LAMB, CHARLES BANKS & CO., JOHN LOVE, DAVID MC-
CREDIE & CO. In the auction and brokerage business,
were PETER TREZEVANT, WILLIAM SKRINE, TRAVERS
ROBERTSON, COLCOCK & PATTERSON, JACOBS & CONYERS,
JACOB DE LEON, JOSEPH PARK, JACOB COHEN, JOHN

POTTER, J. S. CRIPPS, DENOON, CAMPBELL & CO. The co-partnership of NORTH & VESEY was announced as dissolved.

In the number of March 28, 1797, there is a list of American vessels, with the names of their Captains, and the valuation of their cargoes, which were captured by French privateers and gun boats, and sent into different ports in the Island of St. Domingo. As it may be of interest and prove quite serviceable at some future day, a list of them is appended:

May 12.—Schooner Amelia, Cochran, of Boston; cargo, $16,000.

August 11.—Brig Freemason, Wise, of New York; cargo, $26,000 ; vessel, $4,000.

August 20.—Brig Brutus, Aborn, of New York; cargo valued at $10,000; vessel at $5,000.—Schr. Benessoff Parcal, Boniveta, of St. Thomas.

August 26.—Brig Kerren Hannish, Lillebridge, of Philadelphia; cargo, $12,000.—Brig Franklin, Pick, of Philadelphia; cargo, $5,430 ; vessel, $4,000.

August 27.—Brig Mary, Boyle, of Baltimore; cargo, $6,000 ; vessel, $6,000.—Brig Clio, Ball, of Baltimore.

August 31.—Sloop Honor, Kimball, of New London; cargo, $3,000 ; vessel, $1,500.—Sloop Leader, Warner, Cape Ann; cargo, $5,000.—Brig Polly, Watson, of Philadelphia.—Brig Nymph, Sullivan, of Philadelphia; cargo, $10,000.

September 1.—Brig Pearl, Webb, of New London; cargo, $6,000.—Schr. Three Friends, of Baltimore.—Schr. Hodges, Jacocks, of Philadelphia; cargo, $8,000.

September 4.—Schr. Charming Polly, Pritchett, of Baltimore; cargo, $25,000 ; vessel, $3,600.—Sloop Nelly, Adams, of Boston.—Schr. Somerset, Dillingham, of Charleston.—Schr. Catharine, Stoy, of Philadelphia.—Schr. Rainbow, Howland, of New Bedford.

September 17.—Brig Nancy, Mey, of New York; cargo, $20,000; vessel, $5,000.

September 21.—Schr. Anna Maria, Wilson, of Baltimore; cargo, $5,000; vessel, $4,000.

September 23.—Schooner Wilmington Packet, Francis, of Charleston.

Those without dates, are: Brig Pomona, of Baltimore; Brig Experiment, Hutson; Brig Triton; Schr. Hannah; Schr. Nancy; Sloop Sincerity, of Philadelphia; Sloop Delia; Schr. Hibernia; Brig Charlotte; Brig Glasgow, of New York; Schr. ——, of Georgetown; Sloop Joanna, of Providence; Sloop Polly, of States Island; Schr. Eliza and Schr. Three Friends, of Charleston; Schrs. Liberty and Juno, of Boston; Brig Despatch, Lunt, cargo, $8,000; vessel, $4,000; Brig Wolwich, McCutcheon, and Schooner Success, of Philadelphia; Schr. Harding, of New York. There are nine more condemned at L'Anne a Vease, the names of which are not mentioned. L'Anne a Vease, is, doubtless, intended for l'Anse á Veau, an anchorage in the French part of the Island of St. Domingo.

There lived and flourished about this time, (1797,) Mr. JOHN GEYER, one of the merchant princes of the day. He built and owned what was then considered the fire-proof range of stores, at the North East corner of our present North Commercial Wharf; that and the one South, were then known as GEYER'S wharves. The residence of Mr. GEYER, still standing, was, in those good old times, the scene of many elegant hospitalities; and within a few years, there were living those who well remembered this current interrogatory: "Who dines with GEYER to-day?"

JOHN GEYER deserves mention as a man of great energy and success, as a large planter and successful merchant.

He became financially involved by the capture and condemnation of his ships by French privateers, in 1797 and
'98; among them were the ships *Ruby*, the *Rising Sun*,
and the *Rainbow*. He died, February 12th, 1825, at his
residence, No. 10 Atlantic Street, (then Lynch's Street,)
where a grandson of his now resides.

The *South Carolina Gazette and Timothy and Mason's
Daily Advertiser* changed its title and proprietorship in
January, 1806, then B. F. TIMOTHY published it alone, as
the *South Carolina State Gazette, and Timothy's Daily
Advertiser*.

CHAPTER VI.

DAVID R. WILLIAMS, E. S. THOMAS AND OTHER EDITORS—
THE CITY GAZETTE AND DAILY ADVERTISER—THE DAILY
EVENING POST—THE FIFTH DISASTROUS FIRE, OCTOBER,
1810—EARTHQUAKES—SKINNER AND WHILDEN—CRIME
RAMPANT—MR. AND MRS. FISHER—THEIR ARREST AND
EXECUTION—THE SIXTH DISASTROUS FIRE, FEBRUARY,
1835—THE GAZETTE AND ITS EDITORS, FROM 1822 TO
1832—WILLIAM GILMORE SIMMS—THE SEVENTH DISAS-
TROUS FIRE, JUNE, 1835—ABSORPTION OF THE GAZETTE
BY THE COURIER.

DAVID R. WILLIAMS afterwards published the *Gazette
and Advertiser*, and remained proprietor until September,
1809. At the expiration of that year, FRENAU & WILL-
IAMS became the proprietors, and issued the *Gazette and
Advertiser* from the central house of the buildings on East
Bay, now known as "Prioleau's Range."* This range

---

* Opposite to this range of buildings is the office of the Charleston Daily
News, which site was, previous to 1800, known as "Harris' Tavern." Subsequent to Harris' time, a wholesale crockery importing store was kept
there, by one Mr. Allen. After the premises had been closed some years,
they were re-opened as a tavern, and conducted by Lawrence Durse; then
by Orren Byrd, up to 1823; then by Horatio Street, who became manager
of the Planters' Hotel. Louis Eude succeeded Horatio Street It was afterwards successively conducted as the French Coffee House, by R. Mignot,
A. Ligniez, Wm. Greer, and P. J. Coogan. This tavern, entered as it was
from the street by steps, was a resort on Sunday, between 12 M. and 1 P. M.,
for merchants and influential men of that period. It was Mr. Ligniez who,
about the year 1835, substituted for the old front the one more modern in
appearance.

In a small brick building next North of the French Coffee House, George
Lyon, watch-maker and jeweler, was atrociously and mysteriously murder-
ed, on the night of June 11, 1844.

of buildings was, in 1806, known as the "Corner of Commerce," and was constructed by BENJAMIN PAUL WILLIAMS, at a cost of 4,000 guineas, for the storage of produce.

DAVID ROGERSON WILLIAMS, one of the proprietors of the *Gazette*, and who was born 10th March, 1776, was a brother-in-law of the editor, JOHN MCIVER. He was not a man of yesterday, but a genuine exemplar of Carolina honor, firmness and candor. In politics, a tried democrat of the old school—opposed to Federal usurpations—well disciplined in the politics of JEFFERSON and of MADISON. He was a Brigadier General in the regular army, and resigned his commission to take a seat in the United States Congress of 1811 and '12. He retained to the day of his death, the name of " thunder and lightning WILLIAMS," a *sobriquet* obtained after a speech, delivered with all the vehemence of animated rhetoric, in that Congress, against the government of Great Britain.

A letter from Washington, which appeared in the *Courier*, dated January 7, 1812, says :

" Mr. WILLIAMS of your State, spoke above an hour, and " acquitted himself in a manner far beyond my expecta- "tion." Another letter, written by the reporter of the *Baltimore Democratic American*, in alluding to Mr. WILLIAMS' speech, said : " No man can conceive the impressive " manner in which it was delivered, nor the Roman energy " and overwhelming vehemence of the speaker's elocution. " You have seen and heard COOPER. The voice of Mr. " WILLIAMS is more vigorous, more powerful, more com- " manding than that of this celebrated Tragedian."

Mr. WILLIAMS was, in the year 1814, called to the Gubernatorial chair of this State. The courier who was charged with the delivery of the letter which made known to General WILLIAMS his election to a position, in those days acquired without bribery and corruption, met the

General in his wagon on the high road, while he was returning to his house, near Society Hill, from Fulwyder's foundry, on Cowder's Creek, in North Carolina, with machinery for his plantation.

Governor WILLIAMS met with a fatal accident on the afternoon of the 15th of November, 1830, by the falling of a beam, while superintending the building of a bridge over Lynch's Creek. On being relieved from his distressing situation, it was found that both legs were broken below the knee. This caused his death on the following morning at 4 o'clock. He was buried in the cemetery of the family, four miles below Society Hill.

"Even in his ashes live his wonted fires."

In January, 1811, PETER FRENAU & Co., became the proprietors and publishers of the *Gazette and Daily Advertiser*, and held possession until the 1st January, 1812. From that time until January, 1814, Mr. FRENAU'S copartners, SAMUEL J. ELLIOTT and SAMUEL RICHARDS, two very practical typographers, conducted the paper.

PETER FRENAU was a graduate of Princeton College; was versed in the ancient and modern languages, and possessed a wide range of general knowledge. He was the brother of PHILLIP FRENAU, who was the poet of the revolution, and the author of political satires on Royalists— " The House of Night," " The Beauties of Santa Cruz," etc. The latter perished in a snow-storm, near Freehold, New Jersey, in the 80th year of his age, December 18, 1832. Copies of his works have been preserved by that bibliothecal institution, the " Charleston Library Society.'

The *City Gazette and Daily Advertiser* was, on the 1st of July, 1815, with the patronage of several successful years, transferred to E. S. THOMAS, a bookseller, and published by him at 234 East Bay. Mr. THOMAS was by

birth a New Englander, the son of the author, FREDERICK
WILLIAM THOMAS, and nephew of ISAIAH THOMAS, LL. D.
After severing his connection with the press here, he went
to Baltimore, where he became prominent in Maryland
State politics; thence to Providence, Rhode Island, and
he was finally known as the proprietor and editor of *The
Daily Evening Post*, which was published at Cincinnati,
Ohio. Mr. E. S. THOMAS was the author of sketches of his
own life and times, published in 1840. He died in Cin-
cinnati, on the 22nd of October, 1845, aged 71 years.

The fire of the 9th of October, 1810, fourteen years after
that of 1796, was the next of consequence. The newspapers
graphically noticed it. The *Gazette's* report, on account
of its brevity, is selected:

" The fire broke out in a small house in Church Street,
"between St. Philips' Church and Anson Street. It ex-
"tended as far North as Motte Street. Its course South
"was to Queen Street; through that down to Union Street,
"then into Broad Street. The destruction of the house
"occupied by Mr. CHUPEIN, just West of Union Street, was
"the means of preventing the further extension of the
"flames. The loss of property is supposed to be about
"half a million of dollars. In this fire, one hundred and
"ninety four houses have been destroyed."

The months of December, January, and February, 1811,
and 1812, were remarkable for earthquakes in Charléston,
and were the subject of much comment on the part of the
press. Six distinct shocks were felt 16th December, 1811.
The first, was five minutes before 3 o'clock, A. M., and set
the bells of St. Philips' Church ringing. The second occurred while the Town clock was striking three; this was slight-
er than the first, and continued about twenty-two seconds.
The third, was felt at three minutes before 8, A. M., and
the fourth, at ten minutes after 8 o'clock; the vibratory

motion was East and West; wind North-north-east. Two
more shocks were experienced the same night; one at 11
o'clock, and the other at twenty minutes after 12 o'clock—
being six in two days. On the 24th January, 1812, another
of these agitations occurred; and again on the 4th February. On the 7th of the same month, there were two
more shocks—one just before 9, and the other about 11
o'clock, P. M. The first of these was of half a minute du-
ration; the second, two minutes. Another slight shock was
felt on the 10th February. February 21st, 1812, was set
apart by Council, as a day of humiliation, fasting, and
prayer, at the request of the Reverend Clergy of all de-
nominations, and the citizens were requested to humble
themselves on that day before the Most High, imploring
that He would avert from this land the evils which
threatened it, from the frequent awful visitations which
they had of late experienced.

Charleston was not again visited by earthquakes until
7th February, 1843. A few minutes before 10, A. M. on that
day, two distinct shocks were felt. They were very slight,
though many persons in different sections of the City felt
them sensibly. Another, and the last of these visitations
occurred December 19, 1857. It was described by Professor
L. R. GIBBES, as being more of an agitation of the earth, as
no decided shock or blow was perceived. The motion consisted of a series of horizontal oscillations, increasing gradually in distinctness, and then subsiding somewhat more
rapidly, lasting about six or eight minutes.

January 1st, 1816, *The Gazette and Advertiser*, which
had again been advertised for sale, passed into the hands
of SAMUEL HAVILAND SKINNER and JOS. WHILDEN, under
the firm of SKINNER & WHILDEN, and was published at
244 East Bay, corner of Blake's Wharf, (now Central
Atlantic Wharf.) Mr. SKINNER, for two years before he

became one of the proprietors, conducted the printing, and at intervals the editorial department likewise. It has been said of Mr. SKINNER that he was manly and noble in his bearing, elegant in person, gentlemanly in feeling, and generous to a fault. Mr. SKINNER, together with others prominent among the craft, boarded in the family of Mr. EDWARD SEBRING, who then resided two doors East of his present business locality. Mr. SKINNER was drowned near Cape Hatteras, while on a tour to his home in Connecticut. Mr. WHILDEN was known for five years preceding his joint proprietorship, as collector for the establishment of the *Gazette and Advertiser*. Three years later, January, 1819, the *Gazette and Advertiser* was sold, and it became the individual property of JOSEPH WHILDEN.

It will be necessary, *en passant*, to wander from the chronological record and refer to the beneficial influences the press exerted about this time (1819–20) in the suppression of the vice which existed in the City.

Too frequently, the torch of the incendiary, together with the machinations of the desperado, gave scope for individual condemnation. Not less frequent were the warnings given by the City journals to the authorities to suppress the then existing evils.

This condition of society, bad as it was in the City was much worse in its environs. Gangs of white desperadoes occupied certain houses, and infested the roads leading to the City. To such an extent did these outlaws carry their excesses, that wagoners and others coming into the City were under the necessity of carrying rifles in their hands for defence. Travelers passed these houses with fear and trembling. More dreaded than others of these haunts, was that known as the Six Mile House, occupied by JOHN FISHER and LAVINIA, his wife. State Sheriff, N. G. CLEARY, was forced to move against these highwaymen.

With a number of mounted citizens and detachments from the Charleston Riflemen, Washington Light Infantry, and the Northern Volunteers, he started on the errand of extermination.

The City papers of January and February, 1820, give accounts of the capture of Mr. and Mrs. FISHER. The "Constitutional Court" of 19th January, 1820, had refused to grant new trials to JOHN and LAVINIA FISHER, convicted at the previous Court of highway robbery, and they were sentenced to be hung on Friday, 4th February, following. They were, however, respited until the 18th, on their petition, imploring an opportunity for preparation, and asking but for "time to meet their God." On Friday, 18th, at 2 o'clock, just within the lines, on a hill East of the Meeting Street road, about eight hundred yards North of the street, now known as Line Street continued, JOHN FISHER and his wife met their fate, the former with calmness and composure, the latter with fear and trepidation. Mrs. FISHER appeared, from the time of her arrest, to be under the influence of wrong passions and feelings. It was evident she flattered herself with the expectation of pardon from the Executive. Mr. FISHER, on arriving within sight of the gallows, drew his wife convulsively to his bosom, and speedily nerved himself for the issue. The unhappy wife could not believe it possible that she was so soon to die. She called upon the immense throng assembled to rescue her, and implored pity with outstretched and trembling arms. No scene could be more appalling as the ill-fated pair stood between time and eternity. The platform gave way at a given signal from the Sheriff, then all was hushed and still—that which was mortal had put on immortality.

Denmark Vesey (a free black man) and several slaves,

convicted of an attempt to raise an insurrection in the
State, were executed on the same spot, in July, 1822.

Severe strictures were made by the New York *National
Advocate* against the execution of Mr. and Mrs. FISHER,
from the fact that the account of the robbery, together
with the testimony on the trial, were not laid before the
people.   These strictures on our criminal jurisprudence
were ably refuted at the time, by several writers.

It was on the 4th of October, 1822, that JOSEPH WHIL-
DEN retired.   The *Gazette and Daily Advertiser* was then
purchased by EDWARD CAREW, for JOHN GEDDES, jr., son
of General JOHN GEDDES, who was Governor of South
Carolina, from 1818 to 1820, and elected Intendant of
Charleston, in place of Maj. JAMES HAMILTON, jr., in
January, 1823, by sixty-nine majority, only 535 votes having been cast.   ISAAC HARBY was GEDDES' assistant editor, and devoted all his time and talent to the advancement of the political and literary character of the journal,
in the department he was so well fitted to adorn.   In that
paper, on the 19th of June, 1823, it was mentioned that
the first number of the *Georgetown Gazette* had just been
issued in Charleston.   The subsequent numbers were issued
in Georgetown.   In that place, which was at one time
second in importance in the State, the *Gazette* was published by Messrs. ELLIOTT & BURD.   It is quite probable
that Mr. BURD was a son of J. V. BURD, before mentioned
as having died in 1785.

JOHN GEDDES, on the 5th February, 1825, sold the *Gazette and Daily Advertiser* to JAMES HAIG, a talented son
of one of Charleston's respected mechanics, Mr. DAVID
HAIG.   SIMMS, in his skeleton outline of early authors,
says:

"HAIG entered upon the field of journalism, with a rep-

" utation brought from college. He was a man of ability,
" wrote well in a serious vein, but was deficient in that
" sprightliness so essential to a daily newspaper."

On the 28th of June, 1826, there is narrated in HAIG's
Gazette the serious fire of that year. This fire, the *Gazette*
mentions, "broke out on Saturday morning, in the house of
" Mr. JOHN CONNER, saddler and harness maker, on the
" West side of King Street, a few doors above Boundary
" Street, (now Calhoun Street.). The number of houses
" burnt was upwards of thirty, besides the outbuildings.
" The loss of property is supposed to be considerably over
" $100,000. We are happy to state that no lives were lost,
" which had been apprehended, from the repeated explo-
" sions of powder. A fire broke out in the same spot, in
" the year 1800, in which a Mr. and Mrs. MILLER lost
" their lives. This is the greatest calamity of the kind
" since 1810."

JAMES HAIG sold the *Gazette* to a company of gentlemen
composed of CHARLES JOHN STEADMAN, and others, on
the 17th July, 1828. A son of the late Col. STEADMAN
is now, and has been for many years, a Commander in the
Navy of the United States.

On the 4th of August, 1828, the *City Gazette and Daily
Advertiser* announced that THEODORE L. SMITH would be
publisher for the proprietors. The paper was then printed
in Exchange Street, in the rear of the present "Old Post
Office." SMITH sold the *Gazette* to WM. GILMORE SIMMS
and E. SMITH DURYEA, the publishing firm being SIMMS
& DURYEA, and was so announced on the 1st January, 1830.
This firm adopted as a motto for their paper, the following
quotation from OTHELLO's last speech, when summoned
before the Senate of Venice : "Nothing extenuate, nor set
down aught in malice." Under the sub-title was this
citation : "A Map of Honor, Loyalty and Truth," also from

the immortal SHAKSPEARE.   The office of the *Gazette*
was afterwards removed to the South side of Broad Street,
near East Bay.

It was at this locality on one occasion, during the nullification troubles, that the material of the *Gazette* came very
near being destroyed.   A severe political leader from the
pen of Mr. SIMMS, the editor, brought in front of his
office a large number of persons politically opposed to the
course of the paper, and who had proscribed it for its political opinions.   The excited crowd made threats of violence.
Happily it was prevented through the agency of a few
firm friends of Mr. SIMMS' partner, Mr. DURYEA.   The
most prominent of those who came forward in Mr. DUR-
YEA's behalf was DAVID N. McINTOSH, well known to
many of our old citizens.

WILLIAM GILMORE SIMMS subsequently, (April 9, 1832,)
became sole proprietor of the *Gazette*.   Mr. SIMMS effected a
sale and transfer of his establishment to WILLIAM LAW-
RENCE POOLE, on the 7th of June, 1832.   Mr. POOLE came
from Cheraw, in this State, at which place he was publishing the *Cheraw Intelligencer*, to purchase and secure
the *Gazette*.

The brilliant literary career of WM. GILMORE SIMMS,
LL. D., is well known.   He was born in this City on the
17th of April, 1806.   At one period of his life, he escaped
by only one vote, the responsibilities of Lieutenant Governor of this State.   At the time of his death he stood, in
editorial age, next to JACOB N. CARDOZO, and as an author,
takes precedence in the whole South, as the writer of the
greatest number of works, possessing intense local interest.

In youth Mr. SIMMS acquired a taste for letters ; in early manhood this taste was increased by diligent study,
and when his future was determined on, he went forth
upon the stage of life as a scholar.   An earnest reader,

and, possessing a tenacious memory, he turned these advantages to much account, in both public and private life. As a journalist, he wrote just as he talked, and his conversational powers were very great. None more able, could have been found among the fraternity of editors, and he, too, though only as an amateur, grasped the *composing stick*, and buckled to the *case*, in years more youthful, and whilst the young mind was easily impregnated with new ideas.

Who that knew this *savant*—who that has listened to his counsels—who that has enjoyed his confidence, or the benefit of his society—the brightness of his example, and the richness of his friendship—who among them will refuse their sympathy, or hesitate to give their meed of acquiescence to the foregoing sentiments, expressed by one who knew him well—who loved him much, and who records so imperfect a tribute to the mental characteristics of this great Southern *littérateur*. With him mortality has but yesterday, as it were, put on immortality, and now that he is gone, it is as if some prominent feature which formed the principal object of a landscape, were blotted out; the prospect presents to the mind a void, which the surroundings cannot replace. As the sun went down in repose on the evening of the 11th of June, 1870, so faded from view, gently, calmly, and in that peace which became a great life—one whose friends were numbered by thousands, and whose admirers embraced the world.

Our State owes an incalculable debt of gratitude to his genius, and to that talent he had chosen to employ so nobly through life in perpetuating her history—

"Each age to him its grateful dues shall pay."

E. SMITH DURYEA, the co-partner of Mr. SIMMS, was a practical printer, having served his apprenticeship with Mr. A. E. MILLER, and was quite popular as a journalist.

Scarcely had he reached the age of maturity—to the rich development of those social and tender charities of life, in the future usefulness so peculiarly characteristic of his mild deportment and benevolent heart—when he died. This event occurred on the 25th of March, 1832, in the 26th year of his age. E. SMITH DURYEA was the father of Colonel ROBERT S. DURYEA, Counselor at Law in our City.

Before taking leave of the *City Gazette and Daily Advertiser*, and prior to noticing its absorption by the *Courier*, we propose to refer to the memorable fires of the 16th of February, 1835, and that four months after, 6th of June, 1835.

The one of the 16th February, 1835, broke out at the N. E. corner of State and Linguard Streets; sixty-three houses were burnt. The most distressing feature of this calamity, was the destruction of St. Philips' Church, a venerable structure completed in 1723–4.* Truly, the destruction of that venerable pile must have recalled to its worshipers the words of ISAIAH, when in his lamentations over the destruction of Jerusalem he exclaimed: "Then it was that our Holy, and our beauteous house, where our Fathers praised thee, is burned up by fire!" Twice before had this Church escaped when surrounded by fire. First in 1796. It was again in peril in 1810.

Hard on this misfortune, came the calamity of the 6th June, 1835, which the City journals announced as having originated in a small wooden tenement on the West side of Meeting Street, near Hasel Street. The number of buildings destroyed was estimated from three to four hundred.

---

* Shecut, page 6. Divine Service was first performed in this Church in 1723.

Gospel Messenger, vol. xxiv, chapter xvi, page 37. It was in this year (1723) that the Church, then building, was greatly injured by a hurricane.

Some of them, large brick mansions, but much the larger proportion of them were two story frame houses. At this fire the officers and crew of the United States ship *Natchez*, and the Revenue Cutter *Alert;* the officers and privates of the United States Army, and the Captain and crew of the line ship *Niagara* rendered essential aid.

In the year 1837, the material and good will of this paper, under the name of *The South Carolina Gazette*, passed from the hands of Mr. POOLE, into those of Messrs. A. S. WILLINGTON & Co. The *Courier* firm published it as an auxiliary to their " Map of busy life," until the first of October, 1840, when it was discontinued in consequence of the patronage of the daily and tri-weekly having increased to such an extent as to render the publication of it inconvenient.

CHAPTER VII.

ON the 1st October, 1831, the first number of the *State
Rights and Free Trade Evening Post* was issued at 13
Champney Street, (now Exchange Street, South of the Old
Post Office.) This paper was printed by WILLIAM HENRY
GRAY, for JOHN A. STUART. Mr. GRAY was trained as a
printer in the job office of WILLIAM P. YOUNG; and, at one
time, acted as foreman of the *Patriot*, and was afterwards
the senior of the publishing house of GRAY & ELLIS. Mr.
GRAY, who was a zealous member of the craft, died 2d
October, 1836. The *Post* was a party organ, and was
owned by JAMES HAMILTON, R. J. TURNBULL, R. Y.
HAYNE and JOHN A. STUART. The following extract from
the writings of THOMAS JEFFERSON, was the motto under
the Charleston head of this paper:

"Every State has a national right in cases not within

" the compact (*casus non fœderis*) to nullify of their own
" authority, all assumptions of powers by others within
" their limits. Without this right they would be under
" the dominion, absolute and unlimited, of whomsoever
" might exercise this right of judgment over them."

In November, 1832, JAMES C. NORRIS and BENJAMIN
R. GITSINGER purchased the *Post* from Mr. STUART; the
latter having become the proprietor of *The Charleston Mercury*. The *Post* did not change its politics. It continued
to advocate nullification, and, as some regarded, all its kin-
dred heresies. It expired after it had attained its six hundred and eighty-fourth number. It was, afterwards, revived and published as *The Palmetto Battery*, and was edited
by JAMES WRIGHT SIMMONS, the essayist and poet. This
paper also had a short existence, but during its publication
gave evidence of its ardent devotion to the doctrines of
nullification.

Mr. NORRIS was connected with the *Mercury* as its
book-keeper, and subsequently filled several offices within
the gift of the City Council. He died 18th October, 1854—
the anniversary of his birth day, 62 years of age. His
co-partner, Mr. GITSINGER, was known for several years
as the able and devoted foreman of the *Courier*. The proprietors of this paper reluctantly parted with him when
he quitted their service to assume the duties of Inspector
of Streets, an appoinment bestowed upon him by Council.

By some misadventure, on the 7th August, 1855, while
on the fourth floor of the Job Printing establishment of
Messrs. JAMES, WILLIAMS & GITSINGER, 3 Broad Street,
the last named of this firm, while arranging for the removal
of some material, lost his balance, and fell through a trap
door to the lower floor, a distance of some fifty-four feet.
From this accident Mr. GITSINGER never fully recovered.
He died 12th February, 1858.

JAMES WRIGHT SIMMONS, at one time editor of the *Palmetto Battery*, was born in Charleston. His name is enrolled in the imperishable records of literary fame. Early in life (about 1817) he published "The Exiles Return." His "Memnon" followed. After his repeated contributions to the daily journals and magazines, Mr. SIMMONS went North, and was for some time with MORRIS & WILLIS, of the New York *Mirror;* after that, with Colonel WATSON WEBB, of the New-York *Courier and Enquirer;* was the correspondent from Florida of the New York *Evening Star*, and wrote the "Recollections of the Campaign in East Florida," which received the general meed of admiration for their graceful style, lively narrative of events, and elegant pictures of men and scenery. Mr. SIMMONS went to Galveston, Texas, in 1837 or '38, and was associated with Major WHITNEY, of the *Banner*. He was, afterwards, Comptroller General under Governor LAMAR; then Treasurer of the Republic of Texas. From the Boston press as late as 1852, he published "The Greek Girl," a tale in two cantos, and was, also, the author of an elaborate treatise on the "Moral Character of Lord BYRON." While contributing largely to the press in prose, he wrote many fugitive poems. This poet, essayist, dramatist, and reviewer, died at Memphis, Tennessee, in his 68th year. One only of this ancient family is now living. The mother of Mr. SIMMONS was a Miss HAYNE, and one of the six ladies, near relatives of Colonel ISAAC HAYNE, who vainly petitioned Lord JOHN RAWDON, to save from execution, the life of that distinguished gentleman.

The *Times and Political and Commercial Evening Gazette*, another daily journal, was established by Messrs. COX & SHEPPARD, on the 6th of October, 1800, and printed at No. 167 Tradd Street. As shortly after as the 17th November, of the same year, its name was changed to the

Times, City Gazette and Merchants Evening Advertiser.
On the 16th March, 1801, another change took place in its
title, and it became the property of THOMAS CAMPBELL
COX and his brother-in-law, WILLIAM P. YOUNG, the latter
having a silent interest in the paper. *The Times* was
printed at No. 1 Broad Street. Mr. Cox became sole proprietor of the paper early in 1812. He died in this City
on the 18th October, 1814, and was buried in the grave
yard of St. Philips' Church. Mr. THOMAS SHEPPARD was
from Philadelphia, Pennsylvania. He died in this City,
April 10, 1809, in the 31st year of his age, leaving one
son, our fellow citizen, THOMAS C. SHEPPARD.

Mr. YOUNG was a job printer and publisher, and for
many consecutive years conducted *The Palladium of
Knowledge, or the Carolina and Georgia Almanac*, which
was issued from 44 Broad Street.

The idea of using "The Franklin Head" as a sign for a
book store, was first adopted in this City by Mr. YOUNG.
It has been, subsequent to his death, successively adopted
and used by the late W. R. BABCOCK, at the corner of
King and Wentworth Streets, and more recently by SAM-
UEL FOGARTIE, successor to the late Mr. BABCOCK. It is
now the sign which designates "Holmes' Book House."

The late THOMAS COX YOUNG, and the Revd. THOMAS
JOHN YOUNG, who died October 11, 1852, lamented by the
vestry and congregation of St. Michael's Church, were
sons of the publisher and printer, WILLIAM P. YOUNG.

In January, 1816, Messrs. SKRINE & DUKE became the
proprietors of *The Times*, and at the close of 1818, while
under the proprietorship of Mr. J. C. DUKE, it failed. Mr.
DUKE died in 1824, and T. G. SKRINE, the senior partner
died in this City the same year. Mr. SKRINE was the
father of Dr. T. C. SKRINE, who has also been identified
with the newspaper press of Charleston. The former

owners of *The Times*, Messrs. COX & SHEPPARD, were successful as publishers.

The Investigator was a morning paper, published on Vendue Range, four doors from East Bay, by JOHN MACKEY and JOHN LYDE WILSON.

The first issue of *The Investigator* was on the 1st August, 1812 ; its motto being this quotation from DICKINSON : "Think of your ancestors and your posterity." The principles of the paper were thus defined :

"Independence shall be the leading character of the *In-* "*vestigator*, and with a due regard to decency and deco- "rum, the TRUTH, sacred TRUTH, however hard it may "bear upon public delinquents, shall always find a place "in its columns. Indeed, TRUTH, sacred TRUTH shall be "its Polar Star."

This paper was quite small, measuring only 20 by 26 inches. Its place of publication was, afterwards, changed to 226 East Bay. The firm was JOHN MACKEY & Co. Dr. JOHN MACKEY died December 14, 1831. A mural tablet on the South East corner of Trinity Church marks the spot where his remains were interred. Mr. MACKEY was the father of ALBERT G. MACKEY, the distinguished mason, and fluent and ready writer on Masonic Jurisprudence. JOHN MACKEY, the senior proprietor of the *Investigator*, became involved in a rencounter with the Hon. ROBERT J. TURNBULL, during the war of 1812, in Broad Street, directly in front of the building known as the property of the "Hebrew Orphan Society." Mr. TURNBULL, bitter as an anti-war man, crossed from the South side of the street for the purpose of calling Mr. MACKEY to account for having impugned, in his paper, the position he (TURNBULL) had taken in regard to the war. Mr. MACKEY, on receiving a blow from a cane in the hands of Mr. TURNBULL, clenched with his antagonist. Mr. MAC-

7

KEY, being physically superior, soon overcame his opponent, and had him at his mercy; and his fixed purpose, seemingly, was to take the life of his prostrate political foe. Mr. MACKEY had one knee pressed on Mr. TURNBULL'S chest, while with the right hand he firmly grasped his throat. The venerable and honored ALFRED HUGER, then four and twenty years of age, in all the vigor of his manhood, and whom chance placed in the way, went to the rescue of Mr. TURNBULL. The author has heard Mr. HUGER say, that when he approached the combatants, he found that Mr. TURNBULL was being strangled, and that he then resorted to the same method of throttling to save Mr. TURNBULL'S life. While in the performance of this humane duty, he heard some one, from an upper window of the Court House exclaim: "D—n it, HUGER, let MACKEY kill him!"

On the 28th September, 1812, the size of the *Investigator* was increased about one-third. A "Tory mob" as the editor termed it, attacked the office of this paper on the afternoon of Saturday, 3rd October, 1812. "Tertia" or "Great Primer" was the type used for the *Investigator*. This journal was, subsequently, sold by JOHN MACKEY to ISAAC HARBY, who, in 1817, changed its name to *The Southern Patriot, and Commercial Advertiser.*

JOHN LYDE WILSON, of the *Investigator*, was, in 1822, elected Governor of South Carolina. In 1842, he translated in verse, and published in octavo form, the famous episode of "Cupid and Psyche," contained in the Mythological tale from the "Golden Ass" of Apuleius, and was the author of "The Code of Honor," a pamphlet published from the press of THOMAS J. ECCLES, Charleston, in March, 1838. Mr. WILSON published, in New York, about 1827, the codification of the laws of this State. Governor WILSON, was regarded as an extraordinary man; he was born in Marlboro' County, South Carolina, May 24th, 1784, and was admitted to the bar at Columbia, in 1807. His speeches, political and legal, were always compiled with wonderful arrangement and care. This lawyer, editor and Governor, died in Charleston, February 12, 1849, and was buried with appropriate military honors in St. Paul's Church yard.

CHAPTER VIII.

THE SOUTHERN PATRIOT AND COMMERCIAL ADVERTISER—
ISAAC HARBY—ROBERT HOWARD—JACOB N. CARDOZO—
MARTIN E MUNRO—THE CHARLESTON EVENING NEWS—
JOHN CUNNINGHAM AND HIS COADJUTORS—THE SUN—
EDWARD. SILL—H. L. DARR—A. E. MILLER—JOHN C.
HOFF—THE ROSE-BUD—MRS. CAROLINE GILMAN—THE
RAMBLER—DR. JOHN B. IRVING.

MR. HARBY, after taking charge of the *Southern Patriot and Commercial Advertiser*, associated with him Colonel ROBERT HOWARD, father of our exemplary fellow citizens and cotton brokers, Messrs. S. L. HOWARD & BRO. Mr. HARBY withdrew from *The Southern Patriot and Commercial Advertiser*, on the 6th October, 1822, in favor of Colonel HOWARD, who changed its title to *The Southern Patriot*. Col. HOWARD was, for several years, debenture and abstract clerk of the Customs, and was the proprietor of a Reading Room, located in the second story of the building at the South West corner of Broad and East Bay Streets. This Reading Room was formally opened to the merchants on the 31st December, 1831. To Col. HOWARD does the credit belong of having commenced the publication of the Prices Current or weekly *resumé* of the markets, in tabular form. He died while Naval Officer of the Customs, February 20, 1850, in the 79th year of his age, and was buried in St. Philips' Church yard.

ISAAC HARBY was born in Charleston, November 9, 1788,

He was the eldest son of SOLOMON HARBY, of Georgetown,
South Carolina. Mr. HARBY was fond of controversy, and
had few, if any, superiors. He was a popular essayist,
persuasive orator, and the writer of several dramas. Selections from his writings were made and published in
single octavo, in the year 1829, edited by ABRAHAM
MOISE, of this City. Failing in his efforts, in 1825, to
establish a paper to be called *The Examiner*, Mr. HARBY
left Charleston, in June, 1828, and became a resident of
New York City. The scene of his anticipated success soon
proved the grave of his intelligence. He died in New York
on the 14th December, 1828, and just before he had reached his 40th year. Col. HOWARD sold the *Patriot* to J. N.
CARDOZO, on the 1st January, 1823. Mr. CARDOZO sold
The Patriot to MARTIN E. MUNRO, in April, 1845, and
on retiring from the editorial chair, he took leave of his
patrons in a neat, feeling, and well written valedictory
address. Mr. CHARLES K. BISHOP became the editor of
the *Patriot*, under the management of Mr. MUNRO.

Mr. CARDOZO could not resist the exciting influences
which journalism caused—so to speak, a necessity to his
prolific and astute mind. No sooner had he parted with
the *Patriot*, than he sent forward an order for new type
and an outfit, with which he intended to establish *The
Evening News*. The first number of that thoughtful and
well conducted sheet, appeared on the 1st October, 1845.
His re-appearance as a journalist increased, rather than
allayed the bitterness of feeling which existed between
Mr. MUNRO and himself. It made them warm opponents
in journalism. Both ignored the fact that from the editorial sanctum, diatribes should not emanate. Whatever
differences of political opinion may have existed between
them as public journalists, these could afford no valid reason for the employment of personally reproachful and dis-

respectful terms, in their newspaper contests. Let opposing editors differ—let positions be attacked and defended—assumptions either maintained or refuted—all may be accomplished in that spirit of courtesy which should regulate the intercourse between men. It behooves every editor to bestir himself for his country, and his country's interests. It is equally incumbent upon him to perform the duty in a manner that will reflect no discredit upon his profession, and to keep up an amiable and creditable *esprit de corps*. This duty, no honorable supervisor of a public press should lose sight of. When a public journal is diverted from its proper mission, to that of private disputes and differences, its power becomes greatly weakened and perverted.

In an essay on " *The Courtesies, Duties, and Delinquencies of Journalism*," published in the *Courier*, in the spring of 1867, the author endeavored more fully to define the delinquency here alluded to.

The building at the corner of Broad and East Bay Streets, referred to in a preceding page, has, within the author's recollection, been occupied, first by R. L. BAKER, druggist; by A. JORDAN, an extensive dealer in fruit, segars and willow ware; by AMOS HEAD, in 1844–5, as a book and literary depot; by Messrs. COURTENAY and WIENGES, who bought out Mr. HEAD, and were his successors, and who occupied the site until it was demolished in the year 1853. In pulling down that structure to give place to the imposing brown stone edifice, now the property of Messrs. GEORGE A. TRENHOLM & SON, a portion of the wall fell, on the afternoon of the 13th July, 1853, instantly killing Mr. JOHN JOHNSON, mortally wounding Mr. JAMES MAHER, and slightly injuring other operatives.

From this locality, to Line Street, there was established, 21st October, 1833, a regular line of omnibusses, which re-

turned from each extremity, alternate half hours. Pas-
sengers were "taken up and set down." The fare was
12½ cents, or ten tickets for $1.

Let us revert, however, to our original subject, and turn
over a few additional leaves of history, to catch in their
rustlings, some voices of the past that may wisper tidings
of interest, or awake the slumberings of memory. It was
of Mr. CARDOZO we were speaking. The feeble form of
this able, though most aged of Southern editors, is still to be
seen, and until recently, almost daily in the neighborhood
of his ancient, but now abdicated seat of authority. This
gentleman, so well and favorably known, was born in Savannah, Georgia, on the 17th day of June, 1786. He came
to Charleston with his parents, when about eight years old.
After serving a long apprenticeship at a mechanical employment, he was engaged, for some years, as a clerk in a
lumber yard. Subsequently, he took the position as acting
editor of *The Southern Patriot* under Mr. ROBERT HOWARD.
As an American journalist, he is a recognized authority in
Banking, in Commercial Statistics generally, and in Political Economy. The several papers for which he wrote, and
those which he conducted, at different periods for half a
century, were all distinguished for the able handling of
these important subjects. He is well known also as a frequent and discriminating critic of the drama. The vigor
of his mind, even at the advanced age of 84 years, is
testified in the fact of his being the successful competitor
for the prize essay of the "Charleston Board of Trade,"
which received the commendation of that mercantile body
at their last anniversary, April 6, 1870. Mr. CARDOZO
has returned to his native City and State ; there, probably,
to remain the balance of the few years yet vouch-safed to
him on earth.

MARTIN E. MUNRO, proved indefatigable in his endeav-

ors to sustain his paper, the *Patriot;* but it did not exist
longer than the close of 1848. It ceased then to hold its
place among the papers of the day; as also its auxiliary
The Morning Transcript, leaving the field to *The Evening
News.* Mr. MUNRO was always profuse in his acknowledg-
ments of the services of both his foremen, BARNARD LEVY
and A. DESPORTES.

Mr. CARDOZO sold *The Evening News* to Messrs. BUR-
GES & JAMES, in the autumn of 1847. Mr. BISHOP disposed of the interest he had in the paper, and left Charleston shortly after, for the North, and became connected
with *The Newark Eagle;* and was, for several years,
editor and proprietor of that journal. Since then he has
been connected with the *New York Dispatch, Washington Chronicle,* and *New York Weekly.* The distinguished
jurist, WILLIAM D. PORTER, was then called to the editorial department of the *News.* Early in 1848, WILLIAM
Y. PAXTON, purchased an interest in the paper, and the
firm was changed to BURGES, JAMES & PAXTON. Messrs.
BURGES, JAMES & PAXTON sold the *News* to W. Y. PAX-
TON and B. GARDEN PRINGLE, September 9th, 1848.
From the formation of this co-partnership, Mr. PRINGLE,
who, wielded a ready and easy pen, took upon himself
the editorial responsibilities of the *News,* and under his
auspices the reputation of that journal was ably sustained. Another change was made in this paper of so
chequered an existence. In July, 1850, Mr. PRINGLE
terminated his short editorial career, and B. F. PORTER,
of Alabama, succeeded him as editor, and as a member of
the firm of W. Y. PAXTON & Co. Judge PORTER was a
graceful and discursive writer, familiar with literature
and politics, as well as with law. The *News* for a while
enjoyed the editorial labors of that most popular Southern
poet and author, PAUL H. HAYNE. Mr. HAYNE, whose

name has added so much to the literary reputation of
the State, finally took active charge of the literary department, whilst that of the general business devolved on
Mr. PAXTON. W. Y. PAXTON, who had been connected
with the paper about seven years, withdrew from it September 29th, 1855, on account of ill health. Mr. PAXTON'S
interest was taken by Col. JOHN CUNNINGHAM and STE-
PHEN E. PELOT. *The Evening News* suspended early in
the spring of 1861, Col. JOHN CUNNINGHAM, with his com-
positors having gone to Vinegar Hill, Morris' Island, in
defence of Charleston. The paper was resumed on the
return of Col. CUNNINGHAM and the workmen, and it re-
appeared May 1st, 1861. It died shortly afterwards under
the proprietary title of JOHN CUNNINGHAM & Co.; the
silent partners being JAMES B. O'REILLY, and FRANCIS
J. GREEN. STEPHEN E. PELOT withdrew what interest
he had, but a short time before the suspension of the paper.
JAMES S. BURGES, of the firm of BURGES & JAMES, the
second proprietors of the *News*, died in Aiken, South Carolina, on the 21st February, 1850. Messrs. JAMES, PRIN-
GLE and PELOT are now to be found in other spheres of
life. Mr. PAXTON has removed to Sumter, S. C., and has
become the business manager of *The Sumter Watchman*.

JOHN CUNNINGHAM, the spirited journalist, and once
the enthusiastic politician, has bid adieu to both arenas,
and is now known only in the quiet pursuits of domestic
life, at his homestead, in one of the upper Counties of this
State. It was with this paper that our fellow-citizen, A.
C. MCGILLIVRAY was for a time connected as reporter,
besides having been for many years identified with various
departments of the *Patriot, Sun, Standard* and *Daily
News*.

The Sun, a morning paper, was established September
30, 1850, by Messrs. SILL & DARR. The subscription

was, four dollars per annum, ten cents per week, and two cents per single copy. Dr. EDWARD SILL retired from the *Telegraph*, which he was publishing at Columbia, South Carolina, and came to Charleston from our Capital. The " right hand of fellowship" was cordially extended to both himself and his partner, by the press of the City. Mr. DARR is quite practical, and is known to the craft generally. He was business manager for the paper, and likewise its foreman. The mechanical appearance of *The Sun* was neat and tasteful, reflecting credit on the junior partner. During its short career, it was edited at different times by Dr. A. G. MACKEY, EDWARD SILL, jr., PAUL H. HAYNE, and finally by Dr. T. C. SKRINE, who remained its assistant editor until the paper was discontinued, which was on the 28th June, 1851.

Though Mr. CARDOZO stands at the head of the editorial record, there are not to be found among the disciples of FAUST, older representatives than ARCHIBALD EDWARD MILLER and JOHN CRAMER HOFF, now living in this City.

A. E. MILLER, was born in Shelburn, Nova Scotia, 13th April, 1785, and arrived in Charleston, in 1792. He was apprenticed to Messrs. HARRISON & BOWEN, before mentioned as publishers in this City, from 1794, until October, 1804.

Mr. MILLER, after having served a portion of his apprenticeship with HARRISON & BOWEN, continued it in the printing office of WILLIAM P. YOUNG, until October, 1804; then finished a service of eleven years with G. M. BOUNETHEAU. Mr. MILLER took position as foreman of the *Courier* under MARCHANT, WILLINGTON & Co., succeeding a Mr. KENNARD, of Portsmouth, New Hampshire, and who had died on 12th September, 1807, of yellow or strangers' fever, in the 29th year of his age. Mr. KENNARD had endeared himself to his acquaintances by the suavity of his manners, and the correctness of his principles, and to his employers, by his industry. After having held the position of foreman of the *Courier* for nine years, Mr. MILLER established himself in the book and job printing business, on the 2d November, 1816, and became eminent as a publisher. Ever since that period, he has been the proprietor of *Miller's Planters' and Merchant's Almanac.* Among the earliest of the works published by this veteran printer, was WILLIAM GILMORE SIMMS' second book of poems—"Early Lays." SAMUEL K. WILLIAMS, favorably known to the craft, HENRY S. GRIGGS, and JAMES W. McMILLAN, (nephew of W. L. POOLE, once publisher of the *Gazette*,) are the only survivors of those who were, from time to time, apprenticed to Mr. MILLER.

JOHN C. HOFF was born in Philadelphia, in the State of Pennsylvania, March 7, 1795. After he came to Charleston, he was apprenticed in the year 1807 to his uncle, JOHN HOFF, a book-binder and printer. Early in the year 1818, Mr. HOFF worked as a journeyman compositor in the *Courier* office. He went to Savannah in the autumn of 1819, and worked in the same capacity with Messrs. T. S. FELL and ALEXANDER McINTYRE, under the firm of T. S. FELL & Co.. They were then the publishers of *The Savannah Republican*, a journal, by one year, older than *The Charleston Daily Courier.*

In Savannah, Mr. HOFF remained until the close of 1821, when he was recalled to Charleston by his uncle, JOHN HOFF, and continued with him until his uncle's demise, which took place in Philadelphia, in 1826. PHILLIP. HOFF then took charge of the business, and conducted it until he died. Mr. JOHN C. HOFF, succeeded Mr. PHILLIP HOFF, who was also his uncle, at the stand in Broad Street, next East of the Bank of Charleston, and, until 1858, carried on the book and job printing and stationery business, which was inaugurated by his senior uncle, JOHN HOFF, forty-five years before.

The Southern Rose-bud, B. B. HUSSEY & Co., publishers, was a semi-weekly paper. Mrs. CAROLINE GILMAN was the originator of it. Mrs. GILMAN was born in Boston, and her maiden name was HOWARD. This talented lady, feeling the importance of giving to the youthful mind a right direction, formed the plan of issuing a journal for the young. This daughter of " Modern Athens," distinguished more particularly for her prose writings, carried a design so commendable, into effect, in September, 1833. The *Rose-bud* was known from that time, and it was the sprightliest of the ephemeral publications of Charleston. Well received, its character was elevated to the standard of a highly influential literary newspaper. Its name was, in September, 1835, changed to *The Southern Rose*. BURGES & JAMES were the publishers at that time. In this paper, Mrs. GILMAN, who was the editor and author of a work entitled " The Poetry of Traveling in the United States," published some of her best poetry, and most of her prose writings.

The Rambler and *The Bouquet* were also short lived papers, though the former was a very sun in the literary firmament. This fact causes it to be referred to particularly. *The Rambler* was devoted to Reviews, Essays, Tales and Poems. Messrs. MILLER & BROWN were the publishers. *The Rambler* died March 30, 1844. The elegant and easy writer, Dr. JOHN B. IRVING, toiled unceasingly while presiding over its finances, and over its editorial columns.

Dr. IRVING was born in Charleston, and was sent to England by his parents, in the early part of the present century, for the further benefit of his education. He has thus written of his early life :

8

"My college life, which began at Cambridge, in 1808,
"was full of incident. I have chapter after chapter, in
"my diary of things in general, but of racing in particular.
"During my college term, my proximity to New Market,
"that great Metropolis of the Turf, was an irresistible
"temptation to me to indulge my passion for the sport
"that did most easily beguile me. I could not resist my
"propensity that way. It seemed to grow with my growth,
"and strengthen with my strength. I often, in my mo-
"ments of youthful levity, used to laugh and say, if I only
"devoted to my college studies the time I did to acquire a
"thorough acquaintance with the "Stud Book," and a
"familiarity with pending racing events, and their proba-
"ble results, I could not fail to become a very accomplish-
"ed scholar ; the pride and ornament of any University :
"but this alas! was not to be. I was stable-minded, it is
"true, but not stable enough. Like REUBEN, unstable as
"water, I could not excel."

Dr. IRVING has been a miscellaneous writer all his life.
He has contributed a great deal to our daily press, and
frequently edited the *Mercury*, in the absence of the proprietor, Mr. PINCKNEY. It can truthfully be said, that in
his manifold literary writings, he has never indited a word
calculated to injure, or to give pain to any human being.
Dr. IRVING is graceful in elocution, has command of chaste
and beautiful imagery—exquisite humor, pungent, yet
playful satire, and touching pathos. These endowments
have repeatedly brought tributes of applause from large
audiences in this City and elsewhere. His lectures on
COLERIDGE's "Devil's Walk," and "Cock Robin," give evidences of his grace, originality, and happy vein. "A Day
on Cooper River," proves him to be a remarkably spirited
cicerone.

The circumstances which induced Dr. IRVING to prepare

and deliver the lecture on "Cock Robin," which has been declaimed thirty-four times, and which has benefited the charities of life to an amount not less than $11,000, is mentioned as a pleasing episode. The "Literary and Philosophical Society of South Carolina," over which that pure divine, and learned ornithologist, Reverend JOHN BACHMAN, D. D., presided, found, after the completion of their museum, that their revenue was inadequate to compensate the naturalist and chemist, Doctor FELIX LOUIS L'HERMINIER, member and correspondent of several learned societies, who was especially brought from Europe for this service. It was then determined that this want should be met by means of a course of lectures, to be given by some of the prominent members of the society. Doctor IRVING was one of the lecturers, in aid of that fund. "Cock Robin" was the Doctor's theme.

> "'Tis a history
> Handed from ages down ; a nurse's tale."

The simplicity of the subject was relieved by the general splendor of the production, and from every part of the "Old Theatre," on the night of the lecture, rang out universal applause, revealing to the author the pleasing assurance, that from a simple nursery tale, he had drawn compliments from a large and delighted auditory. Dr. IRVING now quietly enjoys communion with thoughts pure and worthy, at his country seat, "Kensington," in St. John's, Berkley, unalloyed by the promiscuous admixtures of City life.

CHAPTER IX.

OF the several rivals now contending for the honors and
rewards held out in Charleston to the press, *The Charleston Daily Courier*, let it be remarked, has had an existence
of sixty-seven years. This fact is only referred to now, as
indicating and measuring, not so much its claims, as a
competitor, but to show what should be its inducements and
motives to grateful remembrance and continued exertions.
The field is ample, both for duties and rewards, and it is
pleasing to state, that in the progressiveness of enlarged
and liberal views, it is fast coming to be admitted, that in
the legitimate and honorable publishing business, the over-
throw of *one competitor* is never necessarily the advancement of another.

The Charleston Daily Courier has outlived all its elders,
and many of its contemporaries in journalism, and in the
history of the press, no less than in other provinces of
thought, action, and adventure, it has witnessed many
changes. These changes constitute a narrative within themselves; which, did space permit, it would be exceedingly
interesting still further to dwell upon.

The *Courier* began its commercial career on the 10th day of January, 1803, sixty-seven years ago, through the energy of AARON SMITH WILLINGTON. This gentleman was born in the Town of Weyland, Massachusetts, on the 12th March, 1781. In 1802, just after reaching his majority, he came to Charleston. It was at the pressing solicitations of LORING ANDREWS, also of Massachusetts, that Mr. WILLINGTON, the friend of Mr. ANDREWS, came to dwell in the Southern quarter of the Union. Mr. WILLINGTON'S purpose was to superintend the mechanical department of a paper that Mr. ANDREWS intended to establish, to supply the place of the *South Carolina State Gazette;* a journal which had just finished its career, in the family of newspapers. These gentlemen, on their arrival in Charleston, found another candidate for newspaper honors, in STEPHEN CULLEN CARPENTER. Mr. CARPENTER was an Irish gentleman, advantageously known as having been, at one time, a writer for the periodical press of London; reporter of the parliamentary proceedings, during the trial consequent upon the impeachment exhibited against WARREN HASTINGS* by the English Government, which began in the spring of 1788, and the author of the "Overland Journey to India," under the assumed name of DONALD CAMPBELL. Mr. CARPENTER was a federalist in politics, and quite active in arranging for the establishment of a political journal. At that time, an effort made to maintain *two* daily papers would, in the opinion of those interested, terminate in the failure of both. Wisely was it, then, that Messrs. ANDREWS and CARPENTER determined to combine both enterprises. This adjustment produced the *Charleston Courier*, on the day already mentioned, from

---

* Warren Hastings, at the conclusion of the speech made by Edmund Burke on that occasion remarked: "I thought, for about half an hour, that I was the greatest villain in the world."

their office, No. 6 Craft's South Range, (Adger's South Wharf.) The tri-weekly, or country edition of this paper was not instituted until April 16, 1804.

In the first number of the *Courier* is the "Prospectus," one column in length. We find, as prominent articles among the reading matter, Congressional proceedings; an epitomized comparison between the monarchical and the consular despotism of France; British domestic intelligence; miscellaneous matter, and a lengthy editorial on the subject of "Intolerance." It concludes with the annexed significant paragraph, in which are occurrences the editor seemed to have anticipated, and which have since come to pass:

"Against the worst of abominations and mischiefs, with "which this growing spirit of intolerance if not resisted "must ultimately overwhelm and trample down the coun- "try, unhinge the public policy, corrupt the morals and "brutalise the manners of the people, and extinguish all "the decencies and tender charities which invigorate, while "they soften the human heart, we shall in some future "number endeavor to warn the citizens of the United "States. To moderate, not to inflame—to mediate and "heal, not exasperate—to fill up the hideous gulph which "now yawns across the commonwealth dividing one por- "tion of the people from the other, shall be the object of "our strenous efforts as it is of our most anxious wishes. "Were the former as potent as the latter is sincere, there "would soon be in this country but one heart, one hand, "one sentiment, and one voice—and that voice would pro- "claim to the world—America is, and ever shall be a "Confederated Republic."

In the advertising columns of this first number, there are the sales at auction advertisements of VEREE & BLAIR, DAVID LOPEZ; SCOTT, CAMPBELL & CO.; WM. HOLMES &

Co.; WM. HORT, and CHARLES LINING, executors, who advertised for sale the lands belonging to the Right Reverend Doctor SMITH. JNO. GILLIS, who offered five dollars reward for JOHN WILLIAMS, a runaway from the schooner *Garland*. Among the most prominent of those who conducted the grocery business, were CROCKER & HICHBORN, THOMAS & FLECHER, JOSEPH WINTHROP, J. M. DAVIS, and McKENZIE & McNEILL. Of the vessels ready for London and Liverpool there were eight; for freight or charter, five, and were advertised by J. WINTHROP, CROCKER & HICHBORN, TUNNO & COX, J. & J. HARGRAVES, BAILEY & WALKER, DAVID McTAGGART, GILLESPIE & MACKAY, W. & E. CRAFTS, JOHN HASLETT. NATHANIEL INGRAHAM advertised for sale "the house the subscriber now resides in, situated in King Street, near South Bay." W. WIGHTMAN had a column advertisement in this first number, and therein announced, "an elegant and fashionable assortment of sterling plate, gold and silver watches, rich jewelry, plated goods, etc." The marine news consisted of six vessels arrived, and five sailed.

In the same issue, there is given an account of the proceedings of Congress, of December 23, 1802, in which is a message from Mr. JEFFERSON, then President, giving information with regard to the violation of the treaties with the United States on the part of Spain, and conveying, among other papers, letters from our consul at New Orleans. Since then the territory of France and Spain on this continent, has not only been ceded to the United States, but also out of that territory great and powerful States of this Union have been formed. The *Courier* has seen in the course of a life of sixty-seven years, nations rise and fall. It chronicled the triumph and descent of the first Napoleon. It announced the trampling by France upon Germany. Events have indeed taken a turn. Germany has been avenged, her hosts have heavily pressed the soil of France. It recorded the first notes of secession which were sounded in New England by JOSIAH QUINCY, and by the Hartford Convention, and it subsequently heard New England's denouncement of State Rights in every shape and form. It mentioned the fact that New England slavers brought Africans to Charleston for sale, and subsequently reported New England's condemnation of the very act inaugurated by herself, and through which she had acquired wealth. It lived in the times which enabled it deservedly to extol such men as WASHINGTON, JEFFERSON, MADISON, MONROE, ADAMS, CHEVES, RUTLEDGE, LOWNDES, CALHOUN, WEBSTER, and CLAY. It lives to-day to herald with deep humiliation, the workings of a self aggrandizing President like GRANT, politicians like MORTON, and Governors like BULLOCK, HOLDEN and SCOTT.

In literature, it has seen the rise and success of COLERIDGE, WORDSWORTH, Sir WALTER SCOTT, COWPER, BYRON, TENNYSON and MOORE, among English Poets; Sir WILLIAM HAMILTON, the HERSCHELLS, HUMPHREY DAVY, and Sir DAVID BREWSTER, among English Philosophers; DICKENS, BULWER, THACKERAY and GEORGE ELIOT, among English Novelists; HALLAM and MACAULEY, among English Historians. It has seen the genius of the new world begin with nothing of value, yet produce such men as WHITNEY, WASHINGTON IRVING, POE, BRYANT, COOPER, KENNEDY, BANCROFT, and our own SIMMS.

American art was then unknown. How is it to-day? The works of ALSTON, BENJAMIN WEST, STUART, FRASER and BOUNETHEAU, reply. Others, too, we might mention, have won admiration from all who love the beautiful and admire genius.

The subsequent publishing localities of the *Courier* were at No. 1 Broad Street, to which place it was removed May

7th, 1806 ; then to No. 28, North side of Broad Street, just West of State Street; then further East, and near the Bay ; then on the South side of Broad Street, West corner of Gadsden's Alley.   There, it was published during the second war with Great Britain, which lasted from 1812 to 1815.

The *Courier* when first issued, had for its superscription, "Printed by A. S. WILLINGTON for LORING ANDREWS." It was printed on paper of demy size, 19 by 22 inches, each page containing four columns; dimensions very circumscribed, when compared with the "Map of busy life," which is now spread before the public.   In its early numbers, there was marked reticence of the publishers on personal or local matters.

It is a fact highly creditable, and worthy of mention, that in all cases of emergency in former days, the merchants—a class of men high-toned and indefatigable in business, free, open and generous in their manner of conducting it—together with the astute politicians, invariably came forward to the aid of our City press, not leaving editors to sustain a cause alone.   In all such cases, the press of South Carolina, more so perhaps than elsewhere, poured forth a profusion of intellect.

Co-eval with the early issues of the *Courier*, there was brought to light one of the most novel attempts at robbery, ever known in Charleston, and which produced much excitement at the time.   The circumstances of the case— known as the "Ground-mole Plot"—were familiar to two, now among the most venerable of the citizens of Charleston, who then, with young and eager eyes, witnessed the scene.   From notes made by one of them, entitled, "Occurrences of my early Life," the *modus operandi* of the would-be bank robber is taken and thus related : The gentleman, then an apprentice to a mechanical concern, was attracted to the scene by the wide-spread rumor, and informed that there had just been dug out from the earth, a human ground-mole, who was industriously attempting to rob the South Carolina Bank, then located in the building now occupied by the Charleston Library Society, at the North West corner of Broad and Church Streets. The man—WITHERS, by name—was discovered in the effort, and arrested before he had effected his purpose. He was of middle size, and had, as his accomplice, a youth, who made his escape. WITHERS was arraigned for this attempt to plunder, but not having accomplished his design, was released from confinement. The examination of this case showed that he came from the West, and that he had visited the City with a drove of horses, and having disposed of them, unfortunately lost all his proceeds by gaming. Desiring to recover his losses, he conceived the idea of so doing, at the expense of others. A project entertained by him was carried into effect one night in October, 1802, by his entering the drain at the intersection of Broad and Church Streets, which, under the old system of drainage, could be entered by the removal of an iron grating. Once in, he tunneled a passage to within a short distance of the bank vault. The strangest part of his feat was, that he remained earthed for the space of, at least, three months. The discovery of the plot—through the incautiousness of the youth—defeated one of the boldest and most novel methods of tapping the strong box of a moneyed institution, ever brought to light.

Early in the summer of 1805, less than three years after the first publication of the *Charleston Courier*, Mr. AN-DREWS, who had an ardent affection for those sweet heart affinities, known by the name of parent, brother and sister, having resolved to return home, parted with the interest he had in the *Courier* establishment to BENJAMIN

BURGH SMITH. Mr. ANDREWS, before he came to Charleston, was the editor, successively, of *The Herald of Freedom*, Boston, and *The Western Star*, of Stockbridge, Massachusetts. While preparing to return North, he was taken sick, and died on the 19th October, 1805, at the early age of 38 years, having retired from the *Courier* but a few months before. Mr. ANDREWS was gifted to a high degree with all those qualities which make men useful to society, and estimable in private life; his manners, plain, frank, and unaffected, showed sincerity, which he possessed in an uncommon degree. In the cemetery of the Unitarian Church of this City, where mortality ends, but where "there is no death but change, soul claspeth soul," LORING ANDREWS, fourth son of JOSEPH ANDREWS, of Hingham, Massachusetts, was buried, aye, forgotten, save by one fair and faithful hand, whose unceasing duty it is to commemorate the spot. "No flowers so fair, no buds so sweet" as those which bedeck the grave of him, who died so soon after the forming period of life.

In the fall of 1805 the *Courier* appeared, published by BENJAMIN BURGH SMITH & Co. Mr. S. C. CARPENTER was the Company.

It was on the 10th of January, 1806, that Mr. SMITH retired from the firm, in the fourth year of the paper's existence; the firm then became MARCHANT, WILLINGTON & Co. "The Wreath or the Rod" was the motto of the paper, and it was placed under the sub-title.

Mr. SMITH was a federalist in politics. He was remarkable for his wit, as well as his talent. This same position insured good breeding, and a respect for the opinions of others. He was distinguished for a courteous method of expression, now, unhappily, too scantily possessed by the press militant. This gentleman died in Charleston, of country fever, on the 2d day of June, 1823, aged 47 years.

Messrs. Marchant, Carpenter, Dalcho, and Willington, the individual members of the firm, were, also, the editors. In their salutatory address to the public, at that
period, appears the following exposition of their future
course as journalists, to wit : * * * * * " Their labors will
" still be the same ; namely, to maintain the Federal Con-
" stitution inviolate, pure, and uncorrupted, generally ; to
" defend, as far as they can, the cause of Christianity,
" order, and good government, and to oppose every attempt
" that may be made, to pervert the sound principles, or
" contaminate the morals of the community. * * * * * The
" new proprietors have not only pledged themselves, that
" the foregoing is to be simply and unequivocally their ob-
" ject; to which they not only bind themselves, but have
" devised means to bind those who may hereafter possess
" the property of the paper. Support or hostility to par-
" ticular parties, *merely as such*, or to particular men, ex-
" cept as they affect or are affected by the general princi-
" ples, avowed, is entirely out of the scope of their views.
" Abhorrent of personal calumny, or vulgar scurrility,
" they promise that their columns shall never be stained
" by any invective or indecorous allusion that can wound
" the feelings of the most sensitive individual, unless the
" fair, manly discussion of affairs, merely national, shall
" have that effect." Mr. Willington was then, for the
first time, known as proprietor.

On the 1st of November, 1806, this firm published a
weekly organ, called the *Carolina Weekly Messenger*, but
it did not succeed in getting hold of the public mind, and
hence it failed. On the 4th of the same month and year,
the first supplement ever published by the *Courier*, made
its appearance, though these appendices had appeared in
other journals, certainly thirty years before. This supplement of the *Courier* contained an Ordinance of the City,

regulating the City Guard. It was a document of some
length, and signed by JOHN DAWSON, jr., then Intendant.
In that supplement, there was, also, a proclamation from
the Intendant, requiring " all owners and occupants of
" houses within the City, to put one or more lights against
" every window fronting the streets, whenever fire or
" other alarms may occur in the night time."

S. C. CARPENTER withdrew from the firm of MARCHANT,
WILLINGTON & Co., on the 9th of July, 1806, and in the
summer of the same year removed to New York City,
where he bought out *The Daily Advertiser*, published in
that City, and began, on the 1st January, 1807, the publication of a half-weekly, called the *People's Friend and
Daily Advertiser*. Mr. CARPENTER pledged himself in the
prospectus of that paper that " its columns shall never
" inflict an unnecessary, or unprovoked sting, in the heart
" of any individual, nor contain a line to wound the bosom
" of integrity or innocence, or to bring a blush into the
" cheek of modesty." Sentiments truly noble, but seldom
regarded now by journalists. The encouragement this paper received outstripped the expectations of the proprietor.
To Philadelphia Mr. CARPENTER went in 1811, and while
there, became the publisher of a magazine, named the
Monthly Register and Review. In the same year, there
was published in England, in six volumes, duodecimo, the
works of S. C. CARPENTER. They consisted of treatises
upon various subjects : Essays, Moral, Critical, and Historical ; Poems ; Translations and Letters upon interesting
subjects. It is to be regretted that these works cannot be
found, so far as is known, in either of our libraries. Mr.
CARPENTER also started *The Bureau, or Repository of Literature, Politics and Intelligence*, but that Magazine was
not a success. From Philadelphia he went to Washington
City, in the summer of 1818, where he obtained an appoint-

ment as book-keeper for the Quarter Master's Department. This was not accomplished, however, without a change of political sentiment, for he became, at least in profession, a violent republican. Mr. CARPENTER was not without his enemies; and the feeling was so intense against him, that in a published letter from Washington, dated July 26th, to the editor of the Baltimore *Patriot*, he was styled "the notorious STEPHEN CULLEN CARPENTER." He was, the letter adds, "placed in a position to the exclusion of native worth and talent." Several of the clerks declared they would leave the public service, if CARPENTER received an appointment in the office where they were. Mr. CAR-PENTER died in 1820, of a chronic disease, after two years residence in Washington.

There is printed, from the London *Courier* of September 30th, 1806, in *The Charleston Courier* of the 5th January, 1807, the account of the execution of JOHN PALM, by command of BONAPARTE. This murder excited, in a peculiar degree, the attention of the English people. It was a direct blow given to the " Liberty of the Press"—the magician which works wonders—the medium which transforms the night of superstition into the noontide of truth.

JOHN PALM was a book publisher, and for selling a work containing " Free strictures on the conduct of BONAPARTE," was dragged from a city under the protection of Prussia, tried by a military commission, and shot in the Austrian City of Brannau. The conduct of PALM, in vindicating the utility of the press, was most gallant. He was offered his pardon upon condition that he would give up the name of the author. This he refused to do. The opportunity was again offered him at the place of execution; but his reply was, "that he would rather die than betray the author." He was immediately shot. With the view of intimidating others, six thousand copies of the sentence of

the tribunal were circulated over the Continent. In return, several patriots subscribed largely for the publication
and distribution of sixty thousand copies of the letter written by PALM to his wife, from the military prison of Brannau, dated the 26th August, 1806, 6 o'clock, in the morning. In that letter PALM instructed his wife to collect, as
soon as possible, the wreck of his fortune, and with it retire
to America, "in which land," he said, "innocence is still
secure, and patriotism is yet revered."

CHAPTER X.

FROM January, 1808, to January, 1809, though the title
of the paper, the career of which we now record, was the
Charleston Courier, yet the sub-title on the second page,
for the length of time above mentioned, read *Courier and
Mercantile Advertiser*. The *Courier* was, at that time, exceeded only by one or two daily papers on the continent.

PETER TIMOTHY MARCHANT, who was a grandson of
PETER TIMOTHY, withdrew from the paper, January, 1808.
Mr. WILLINGTON and Doctor DALCHO remained, under the
firm of A. S. WILLINGTON & Co.

On the 3d July, 1809, Mr. E. MORFORD, a bookseller,
whose store was the great literary centre of the City, and
who was, as will be seen, the founder of the *Mercury*,
became an associate editor, and one of the proprietors of
the *Courier*, the firm then assuming the title of E. MOR-
FORD, WILLINGTON & Co. This firm established and conducted a Reading Room, second in importance to that established by ROBERT HOWARD, (already noticed) in the City.
They were also extensively engaged in the traffic of patent
medicines, and material appertaining to the book trade.

It was in MORFORD, WILLINGTON & Co's Reading Room that the "Franklin Society," which was established in 1813, held their meetings.

On the 1st July, 1812, the proprietors of the *Courier*, Messrs. MORFORD, WILLINGTON & Co., announced that the paper would be reduced to half a sheet, in consequence of the difficulty of procuring paper. The non-intercourse act produced this abridgment.

The embargo* soon followed. The bill for an embargo of sixty days, was carried in the House of Representatives of the United States, on 3d April, 1812. Having passed the Senate, the bill was ratified by President MADISON, on the 4th of the same month. This was the precursor of determined war, after a peace of nine and twenty years. The President's proclamation supervened. It was declaring a state of war existing between the "United Kingdom of Great Britain and Ireland, and the Dependencies thereof, and the United States, and their Territories," and was dated at Washington, on the 19th June, 1812. War was formally proclaimed in Charleston, in compliance with the President's proclamation, at 12 M., June 26, 1812, by NATHANIEL GREENE CLEARY, Sheriff of the District, "accompanied by beat of drum."

On the 1st October, 1812, the *Courier* resumed its former size, arrangements for a supply of paper having been perfected with a factory in a neighboring State.

The columns of the City papers at this period, December, 1812, are filled with recitals of that distressing catastro-

---

* The embargo was the result of the unsettled differences with Great Britain, and the imperious demands of France. It was a measure of general precaution. John Randolph was said to be the father of it. This inhibition of the departure of our vessels from the ports of the United States, "was removed," Mr. Jefferson has said, "solely to quiet the excitement in New England."

phe, the burning of PLACIDE's Theatre, Richmond, Virginia.

So distressing are the accounts of that calamity, and so great was the lamentation which immediately followed, throughout the States, that a description of an occurrence so tragical in its results, will here be attempted.

Seven hundred persons were estimated as being in the theatre, at the time the announcement was made that the building was on fire. It was the night of PLACIDE's benefit; and the pantomime of the "Bleeding Nun" was being performed. After the fire, which was accidental, one hundred dead bodies were taken from under the ruins; fifty more, it was supposed, were burned up, and many persons were seriously injured. Soon after the terrible event, Mr. PLACIDE wrote to many of the theatrical managers in other cities, earnestly requesting them to alter their theatres, that every facility should be offered to enable the audience to leave such places, speedily, in cases of alarm.

The proprietors of the Old Theatre, situated at what was then the western extremity of Broad Street, West corner of New Street, in this City, acted promptly on the suggestion of Mr. PLACIDE. Such alteration was then made in that structure, as gave thirteen outlets to the large audience, which assembled, not long afterwards, at that popular place of amusement, to witness the performances in aid of that renowned actor.

It was on the 1st June, 1813, during a period of innumerable difficulties, which had their origin in the war, that Mr. WILLINGTON assumed the sole proprietorship of the *Courier*, and aimed at making the paper a commercial and business journal, and rather a medium of general intelligence and literature, than a political organ. Mr. MORFORD, after severing a connection of about four years with the *Courier*, returned, temporarily, to his home in New Jersey.

Dr. DALCHO, who was ordained a Deacon by Bishop DE-HON, 15th February, 1814, and Priest by Bishop WHITE of Pennsylvania, 12th June, 1816, was, in 1819, called to the ministerial charge of St. Michael's Church. This skillful editor was born in London, and came to America when a mere lad. It was in Maryland that his whole education was received. He long adorned the community in which he lived, by his urbanity, literary accomplishments, and Christian virtues. To him we owe several works, among them a history of the Episcopal Church in South Carolina, published in 1820, and which will always continue an authority in local history. The Masonic Fraternity is also indebted to him for an Ahiman Rezon. This sincere Divine, died 24th November, 1836, in the 67th year of his age, and 22nd year of his ministry.

In 1814, the office of the *Courier* was removed to No. 63 East Bay, second door from Broad Street, opposite the North corner of the Exchange. This site now constitutes the North portion, or half of the building which has recently been purchased and remodeled by JOHN SIDNEY RIGGS. The location of the office here, was firmly impressed on the mind of the author, by the occurrence of a shocking suicide. The particulars of that occurrence, which took place September 22, 1835, are here given: ISIDORE GAND-OUIN, an old French inhabitant of this City, kept a small miscellaneous dry goods and hat store, two doors North of the 63 location. It was the North tenement of the building, but recently supplanted by Mr. LITSCHGI'S new building.

On the morning of the day alluded to, between the hours of ten and eleven o'clock, Mr. GANDOUIN discharg·

ed the contents of a heavily loaded horseman's pistol into his mouth, blowing off his head, the lower part of the jaw only remaining. Bodily infirmities, increased by approaching blindness, caused the melancholy refuge, in self-inflicted death. But a few days before he committed the act, he alluded to the painful situation in which he stood, and of his intention. It seemed perfectly intolerable to the combined pride, and honesty of his nature, to battle longer with the ills of life. What was regarded as an empty ebullition of discontent, soon proved a fatal truth.

The specie which belonged to the different banks, amounting, the *Courier* tells us, to " two million, five hundred thousand dollars, arrived in town in wagons, 22nd April, 1816, from Columbia, where it had been deposited during the war." The Christ Church Parish troop, under the command of Captain HIBBEN, escorted the wagon train from Columbia to Charleston.

Mr. WILLINGTON was his own boarding officer, soon after he became sole proprietor of the *Courier*. The duty he performed in an open boat, eighteen feet in length, with width in proportion; sharp bow, square stern, and rowed by two stalwart slaves. From a vessel, boarded by himself outside of the bar, he obtained the positive news of the treaty of peace between Great Britain and America. This information, received as it was from Savannah, on the 11th February, 1815, by express from Fernandina, Florida, was made known, first to Admiral COCKBURN ; then in command of the British Naval force in the Chesapeake and its waters, through a dispatch vessel, a Sweedish pilot boat expressed from Cowes, England. Having obtained this information exclusively, in the manner mentioned, Mr. WILLINGTON announced the fact to his readers, on the morning of the 14th February, 1815. The treaty had been consummated at Ghent, nearly two months before. Tidings

so gratifying were proclaimed that day, says the *Courier*,
" throughout Charleston, by the Sheriff of the District, ac-
" companied by a full band of military music, in a carriage,
" with the Star Spangled Banner of the Union, and the
" Red Cross of Britain united." The event was celebrated
in Charleston, on the night of Tuesday, 28th February, by
the brilliant illuminating of public buildings, and private
residences.

The duties of boarding officer in the early days of the
press, were such as required constant exposure of person,
whilst great energy and perseverance were essential ad-
juncts to its faithful performance.

EMANUEL JONES assumed the duties of boarding officer
after Mr. WILLINGTON. Mr. JONES' constitution became
so greatly impaired through his devotion to business, that
he died September 5th, 1826. JOSEPH PREVOST, who came
to Charleston in the autumn of the same year, then entered
the service of the *Courier*. From 1834, until the close of
1836, THOMAS SAVAGE YOU was Mr. PREVOST's assistant ;
then JOHN GORDON performed the duties of assistant
boarding officer, and continued so to do, until his death,
which occurred in 1846. The office then devolved upon
GEORGE LINDSAY, another of Mr. PREVOST's assistants.

The most formidable of the opponents Mr. PREVOST had
at various times, in this line of business, were SAMUEL
WILCOX, WILLIAM PATTON, WILLIAM G. TRENHOLM and
JOHN G. LA ROCHE, boarding officers, at intervals, for the
offices of the *Gazette*, *Post*, *Mercury*, and *Patriot*. Messrs.
JONES, PREVOST and WILCOX, were, in that line of business, men of indomitable will and purpose.

R. A. TAVEL succeeded Mr. PREVOST, and became
boarding officer and marine reporter for the combined daily press, with Mr. JOHN KNOX, as his assistant. For the
past twenty years, Mr. TAVEL has been one of the most

assiduous of workers in this, as well as in other departments appertaining to journalism.

Mr. WILLINGTON, when about to leave the State in
1819, on his first Europan tour, appointed Mr. ISAAC
COURSE, his brother-in-law, and Mr. JOHN GOODWIN, who
was also a relative, his attorneys; the editorial duties he
confided to Mr. T. G. WOODWARD, and E. P. STARR.

An observatory, erected by J. M. ELFORD, in August,
1822, over his "Navigation School," located at 149 East
Bay, opposite Atlantic Central Wharf, was of great benefit to
the boarding officers of the newspapers, and the Commercial public also. This observatory was so elevated as to have
a commanding view over the bar, and from the middle of
Sullivan's Island, to the then located tower in rear of Fort
Johnson. A signal staff was erected on the South side of
the observatory. When a square rigged vessel was seen
in the offing, a black ball was hoisted; when two or more
were in sight, two black balls were hoisted; for fore-and-
aft vessels, white balls were hoisted in the same order.
The balls were kept up until the vessels came to anchor.
The frame of this observatory was to be seen as late as
1849. Mr. ELFORD was the author of the "Marine Telegraph, or Manual Signal Book," published in August,
1823. This excellent invention of Captain ELFORD grew
into extensive circulation. It reminds us of the fact, by
the way, that the first practical employment of telegraphic
communication between distant points, was by the French
Government, and cannot with certainty be traced to an
earlier period than the year 1793. Flag signals from the
cupola of the Custom House, or "Old Post Office," succeeded these ball signals, and were used to designate the
approach of the Wilmington steamers bringing the Northern mail; at a more recent period the New York line of
steam ships were sighted by means of a strong achromatic

telescope from this cupola full twenty miles at sea, and these signals were hoisted, regularly, in notification of their approach. The death of Captain ELFORD, which took place on the evening of 25th January, 1826, was considered at the time as a loss to the commercial interests of the United States.

CHAPTER XI.

IN the spring of 1821, the *Courier* appeared in its fourth,
and, up to that time, its most approved, new dress. The
title was then changed from *Charleston Courier*, to *The
Charleston Courier*. The motto, "What is it but a map
of busy life," from COWPER'S Winter Evening, and the
quotation for the Poet's Corner, from the pen of WASHING-
TON IRVING, were adopted at the same time. The Hon.
WILLIAM CRAFTS was, at this time, called, for a brief
period, to the editorial charge of the paper. Not only
then, but repeatedly afterwards, the *Courier's* columns
were adorned by his elegant contributions, in prose and
verse. The *Courier*, with the daily editorials of WILLIAM
CRAFTS, assisted occasionally by HENRY T. FARMER, JAS.
CARROL COURTENAY, that vigorous pamphleteer, EDWIN C.
HOLLAND, WM. GILMORE SIMMS, Reverend SAMUEL GIL-
MAN, WM. HENRY TIMROD, THOMAS BEE, and others, was
distinguished for vivacity and variety ; though its prominent object, as a business paper, was not overlooked.

It is quite reasonable to suppose that the motto line,
taken from COWPER, (who was surnamed Modern ISAIAH,)

10

was the suggestion of the talented CRAFTS. The personal history and character, and the peculiar talent of the English poet, had then been bequeathed to all literary and religious enthusiasts. The recollection of what COWPER was, and what he suffered, must have taken strong hold upon CRAFTS, who had all the sensitiveness of a true poetic spirit within him, and could, therefore, appreciate the genius of the British author.

WILLIAM CRAFTS was born in Charleston, January 24, 1787; was admitted to the Sophomore Class of Harvard College in the autumn of 1802; graduated in 1805, and began the study of law at the age of nineteen years. He died at Lebanon Springs, New York, September 22, 1826. His remains were conveyed to his relatives in Boston for interment. HENRY TUDOR FARMER, the chaste and elegant writer, and graduate of Eaton College, penned Mr. CRAFTS' epitaph; fulfilling a promise which had been exacted of him by the deceased, eight years before. Mr. FARMER came from England. While a student, he published a volume, entitled, "Imagination, the Maniac's Dream, and other Poems," which exhibited some strong and beautiful touches of tenderness and pathos, and was issued from the press of KIRK & MERCIER, New York. Other poems also were from his pen. He wrote frequently for the daily press. FARMER survived his friend CRAFTS but three years and three months. His epitaph can be seen in St. Michael's Church yard. Sons of this editor and essayist—C. BARING FARMER, and H. TUDOR FARMER—reside in Walterboro, South Carolina.

It has been said of CRAFTS that "no limit could have "been assigned to his reputation, felicity and usefulness, "had his application been equal to his genius." The only surviving male relative of the late WILLIAM CRAFTS is his

half-brother, our courteous fellow citizen, Captain GEORGE
I. CRAFTS.

It will be mentioned just here, parenthetically, that
about 1823, JAMES GORDON BENNETT, now the most renowned of Northern journalists, became an employé in the
office of the *Courier*. After a few months' residence in
Charleston, he returned to New York, and connected himself with the *Courier and Enquirer*. He issued proposals
in October, 1832, for the publication of *The New York
Globe*. It was published, a short time, in William Street.
In May, 1835, Mr. BENNETT brought into existence the
present *New York Herald*, the second paper of that name
ever published in New York ; a paper which, in its early
career, had the reputation of being the most unscrupulous
journal in the United States. Fame and wealth have,
since that period, marked the career of JAMES GORDON
BENNETT.

A new font of letter again became a necessity with the
Courier, and the edition of 2nd January, 1826, was worked off on a form of new type, which came from the foun-
dery of Messrs. WILLIAM HAGAR & Co., of New York.

Mr. WILLINGTON, in mentioning the fact, stated " that
" the circulation had become so large, as to render it diffi-
" cult to strike it off, with the presses then in common use,
" in the period allowed for that purpose. But it is our
" intention," said the proprietor, " as soon as experience
" shall have tested the advantages of some recent inven-
" tions in printing presses, to avail ourselves of them, in
" order to expedite the printing of our paper."

At the time alluded to, SMITH'S iron press was used in
working off the edition ; ADAMS' power press, with composition rollers, was afterwards, (September 1st, 1834,) introduced and adopted. It gave seven hundred impressions
to the hour. Steam was not applied, in working off the

Courier, until early in 1851, though its proprietors would
have been the first to use it, in working off their paper,
had it not been for the disclosure of the secret order given
by Messrs. A. S. WILLINGTON & Co. to Messrs. CAMERON,
MCDERMID & MUSTARD, early in the year 1849. This
order was for an engine, to be made entire by those ma-
chinists, and which was to be put on exhibition, in competition for the prize, at the first fair of the "South
Carolina Institute." This contemplated advance in the
Courier press-room was not, as it was hoped, smothered up
in silence, and before that piece of mechanism—pretty
and creditable as it was—could be completed, these instruments were imported, and other presses were driven
by steam.

The credit for the adaptation of steam power for printing here, is due to Messrs. WALKER & JAMES, who were
extensively engaged in book and job printing. This firm,
in February, 1850, applied steam to a double medium cylinder machine, manufactured by Messrs. R. HOE & Co., of
New York. The imprint of their firm was "Pioneer Steam
Presses, of WALKER & JAMES, Charleston, S. C." The
first sheets issued through the agency of steam, were
those of a short-lived hebdomadal, issued by this firm, and
edited by W. C. RICHARDS, assisted by PAUL H. HAYNE
and HENRY TIMROD.

Mr. WILLINGTON remained sole proprietor of the *Courier*, until the 1st day of January, 1833, when he associated
with him, as joint co-partners and editors, RICHARD YEA-
DON and WILLIAM S. KING. These gentlemen became,
each, an owner of one portion of the paper, by purchase.
Continued prosperity followed this change. From this
office, the first letter-sheet Prices Current was issued, in
September, 1833.

It is not only opportune, but interesting to narrate here,

one of the grandest celestial sights, ever viewed by man; which account is extracted from the *Courier* of the 14th of November, 1833 :

" Brilliant Phenomenon.*—The atmosphere was on Tues-
" day night last, illuminated with a brilliant and extraor-
" dinary meteoric display. It consisted of myriads of
" falling or shooting stars, even of a large size, darting in
" an oblique direction towards the earth, seemingly from
" every part of the heavens, and occasionally exploding
" like rockets. The luminous appearances commenced
" about midnight, and were most brilliant between 3 and 4
" o'clock, A. M. ; being assimilated, by those who witnessed
" them, to a fiery rain or hail, and continued until sunrise.
" We understand that a very large meteor exploded imme-
" diately over the City Hall. A sudden change of atmos-
" phere from hot to cold, which took place during the
" night, was, probably, closely connected with the origin of
" the phenomenon. We have been informed by Captain
" JACKSON, who was at sea at night, at the distance of nine
" miles from land, that the heavens were illuminated with
" meteors, during nearly the whole night, as far as the eye
" could reach, in every direction ; presenting a spectacle of
" uncommon magnificence and sublimity, attended with
" frequent explosions, resembling the discharge of small
" arms. We learn, also, that a meteor of extraordinary
" size was observed at sea, to course the heavens for a great
" length of time, and then exploded, with the noise of a
" cannon. We trust that a full account of it will be fur-
" nished by some scientific hand."

A very singular occurrence took place in the *Courier*

---

* This remarkable occurrence was witnessed by the author, then a mere boy. Through the thoughtfulness of his father, he was aroused from his sleep, to view a spectacle which he never can forget, and which filled him with fear and admiration.

establishment àfter midnight of the 27th of April, 1835,
which prevented the appearance of the *Courier* in the
morning.   One of the journeyman, SAMUEL F. COLE, was
engaged in justifying the form, after the foreman had
finished "making up," and had left the office; COLE was
left alone with his only attendant, a negro press-hand,
and the latter, as was the custom, had gone for the other
press-hand, two being required to do the labor.   When
the negro returned, he found a large quantity of type on
the pavement, in front of the office, and the remainder of
that which belonged to the form, in most admirable confusion, lying about the "imposing stone."   From appearances, COLE had broken the second page, "locked up" the
other, and lifting it up to the window, precipitated it into
the street, furniture and all; an exertion that required
considerable strength.   Mr. COLE was found, shortly after,
in bed.   On being charged with the commission of the
outrage, he readily acknowledged it, and when asked his
object in destroying that which took so much labor to accomplish, answered, "I did it in masonry," and also said
"it is the want of money."   Some suspicion was attached
to him, as being the person who had set fire to both the
Courier and *Mercury* offices, on the night of Saturday, 4th
of October, 1834.   When charged with this act, he acknowledged that also.   COLE was likewise charged with
setting fire to a residence in Laurens Street, where he
boarded, and which was burned down on the night of the
7th of November, 1834.   When this offence was imputed
to him, he sneeringly replied, "You accuse me of every
thing, you may as well say, I burned down St. Philips'
Church, also."   COLE was committed to the Poor House,
where his father was at the time, confined as a lunatic.

The office of the *Courier* was, on the 3rd of January,
1837, removed from 63 East Bay, to 111 East Bay, just

after the completion of what was then a novelty, even in New York City, its present marble front.

Some idea can be formed of the comparative insignificancy of the mail matter which came into, and went out of Charleston, even up to a period as recent as 1839. On the 15th of November, 1836, consequent upon a change of schedule in the departure of the United States Mail from Fayetteville, North Carolina, the Charleston papers of that day announced that the Government had established a horse express, between this City and the point mentioned. Much interest was manifested by the people of Charleston, at the daily coming in of this express. The carrier would urge his horse, with whip and spur, in his course down Meeting street, through Broad street, and up to the very steps of the Post Office, and there deliver his mails. An accident, which happened to this express on the afternoon of October 14, 1837, will be remembered by many of our citizens. For the purpose of cleaning out a drain which then intersected Meeting and Chalmers streets, an aperture of considerable size was necessarily made. The rider on coming in, the afternoon alluded to, did not discover the opening in time to avoid it, and into the chasm both the rider and his horse went. The rider crawled out, but much injured, but the horse, owing to the injuries received, had to be shot. This express mail was robbed on the night of June 17, 1838, when about forty miles from Charleston. The rate of postage by the express, which was in operation upwards of three years, was 75 cents for single letters, and $1.50 for double letters.

CHAPTER XII.

OF all the fires that had happened in Charleston, that of
the 27th April, 1838, was, up to that period, the most ruin-
ous. It broke out at 9 o'clock at night, at the North West
corner of King and Berresford Streets. The list of houses
destroyed, covered three and a half columns of the *Courier*.
The loss of property was estimated at three millions of dollars ; and the loss of life plunged many of our most worthy
families in the deepest distress. It was greater than at
any previous, or subsequent fire, excepting, perhaps, that
less important one produced by the terrific explosion, at
the depot of the North Eastern Rail Road, at the time of
the last surrender of Charleston, which has been estimated
at from seventy-five to one hundred, mostly negroes.

The conflagration of '38, extended North and East.
Powder was freely used. The firemen having become ex-
hausted, it was hoped that the engineer department, then
in existence, would, by blowing up, put a stop to the
raging element. In blowing up the house which stood at

the South West corner of King and Liberty Streets, Mr.
FREDERICK SCHNIERLE, a prominent citizen, and a member of the department, lost his life. With him perished
Mr. JOHN S. PEART. Colonel CHARLES JOHN STEEDMAN,
(before mentioned as one of the proprietors of the *Gazette*)
was killed, while blowing up a house on the West side of
East Bay, next South of Hasel Street, together with his
attendant, a colored man, named WILLIAM, the property
of Mrs. TAYLOR, a widow. Capt. DUFF, of the ship *Herald*, and Mr. M. F. TURLEY, of this City, sustained serious
injuries.

The services of Mr. J. D. BROWNE, a gentleman well
skilled in pyrotechny, were called into requisition on the
night of that fire. To him was confided the responsibility
of blowing up the houses on the West side of Meeting
Street, from a large wooden building, used as a theatre,
North to Market Street; thence from the South East corner of Meeting and Market Streets East to Church Street.
The proper time-fuses used by the engineers having given
out, they then had to resort to the common port-fire and
kegs of powder. Mr. BROWNE was successfully employed
until he reached the house then occupied by an Italian,
named JACOB GEANNI, midway between the opposite
points. In blowing up that building, he met with his first
injury—a severe gash on the fore-head. This did not de-
ter him in the performance of his extremely hazardous
duty. On he went, toppling building after building, until
he blew up the last house assigned to him, which was just
before midnight. There, he narrowly escaped with his
life, and was, as he has told the author, "literally burnt
from head to foot." His life was, for a long time, despair-
ed of. Mr. BROWNE still lives, but bears the marks received on that eventful night.

The light of this fire was reported as having been seen

at 3 o'clock on the morning of 27th April, 1838, full twenty-five miles South of Savannah, being in a direct line, about eighty miles from Charleston. A piece of burnt linen was picked up on the morning of the fire, by a planter on his place fifteen miles distant, where the light was most distinctly seen, and where the noise occasioned by the blowing up of houses was heard.

The 3d of January, 1853, marked an epoch in the history of the *Courier*. On that propitious day, the semi-centennial anniversary of this journal was celebrated by a banquet given at Butterfields' Pavilion Hotel. At that feast, the "Press-gang" of the City, editorial and operative, were gathered. Mr. WILLINGTON presided, and was assisted, at that grateful and joyous festival, by Mr. YEADON, as Vice-President. The lapse of fifty years found the original publisher of the *Courier*, still at its head, and gracefully celebrating the occasion, in healthful spirits and manly vigor.

At 111 East Bay, for about a quarter of a century, the *Courier* experienced its greatest prosperity. It was in the autumn of 1860, increased in size to 30 by 44, and worked off on two of HOE's single cylinder presses. The paper then used was of domestic fabric, having been manufactured by the "South Carolina Paper Manufacturing Company." That Company had been regularly supplying paper to the concern since December, 1852.

On the 23d February, 1861, the political condition of the country warranting it, there was placed, immediately under the imprint of the paper, the national words, "Confederated States of America."

From 111 East Bay—its present location—this paper daily recorded the upheavings of "Secession," events which were temporarily to reduce the paper to the period of its second greatest trial. It was in close proximity to this site, that a piece of ordnance—known as "Old Secession," obtained by the author from the Spanish Bark *Olympia*, through her consignees, Messrs. HALL & Co., was kept in readiness for the work it was required to chronicle in that momentous drama. From the corner of East Bay and Broad Streets, near midnight on the 10th November, 1860, the discharges from that gun—a six pounder—first announced to the slumbering citizens of Charleston, that the Bill calling a Convention of the State, had just passed the Legislature. That gun which had then begun to play a conspicuous part in the incidents destined to become historical, again, on the 20th December, 1860, pealed forth, almost instantaneously, announcing the passage of the Ordinance of Secession. On that occasion, it stood on the vacant space, to the North of the Exchange, and thence it thundered forth the news, as soon as received, of each State falling into line, in support of the political sentiments of South Carolina. The sons of the soil who were called by the projector, to aid him in consecrating that gun to patriotism, resolved that it should never again be devoted to a common use.

The columns of the *Courier* of the 12th and 13th December, 1861, record a terrible and mysterious dispensation of Providence. We allude to the devastating fire of that year, known as the greatest of all our City fires, in magnitude.

It began in the large sash and blind factory of Messrs. W. P. RUSSELL & Co., near the foot of Hasel Street, about half-past eight o'clock, on Wednesday night, December 11, 1861. The wind, which was blowing strongly from North-Northeast, increased almost to a hurricane. The flames rose to a terrible pitch, and in a few moments, notwithstanding the most gallant efforts of an efficient fire brigade, were communicated to the adjacent workshops and buildings, including the large foundry of Messrs. CAMERON & Co. This was, for the second time, destroyed. By this time the fire indicated the most disastrous results. Building after building caught, and became, as it were, one vast sheet of flame. Furious gusts of wind carried and scattered, in every direction, the burning flakes. Men, women and children were to be seen fleeing from their homes in the greatest distress, and adding much, of course, to the excitement.

From the foot of Hasel Street, on Cooper River, East, to the end of Tradd Street, on the Ashley, running West, the conflagration made a clean sweep of portions of the following streets, and together with these are enumerated the number of sufferers who owned one or more houses: Hasel Street, 6 sufferers; Pritchard Street, 8; Pinckney Street, 19; East Bay Street, 29; Anson Street, 11; Motte Lane, 4; Guignard Street, 7; State Street, 12; Church Street, 18; Cumberland Street, 17; Meeting Street, 33, exclusive of the Circular Church and Theatre; Clifford Street, 7; Horlbeck's Alley, 12; Queen Street, 29; King Street, 50; Broad Street, 21, exclusive of St. Andrew's Hall and St. Finbar's Cathedral; Mazyck Street, 8; Franklin Street, 2; Short Street, 7; Friend Street, 21; Tradd Street, West, 23; New Street, 15; Savage Street, 28; Logan Street, 10, exclusive of St. Peter's Church; Limehouse Street, 4. Thus it will be seen, that there were, at least, 389 sufferers, many of them owning more than one house; buildings, not of wood, but mostly of brick, of good size and appearance. The area of ground was 540 acres, and the loss of property variously estimated at from five to seven millions of dollars. The great fire of 1838, was almost obliterated from the memory of Charlestonians, by this more disastrous one of 1861. It can well be said, that this fire " caused poverty to wring her hands in agony."

11

During the memorable siege of Charleston, the shelling from the Federal fortifications on Morris' Island and its vicinity, which began at half-past one o'clock, on the morning of the 22d August, 1863, had increased to such an extent as to cause the removal of the *Courier* establishment, two months later, out of range of the enemy's shells. For the purpose of this removal, the publication of the paper was suspended Saturday, November 21, 1863, on the one hundred and thirty-first day of the siege, and resumed Monday, November 30, 1863, on the premises of Mr. F. H. WHITNEY, South East corner of Meeting and Reid Streets. But once before, in the long course of over sixty years, has the *Courier* been known temporarily to suspend.

It was at the corner of Meeting and Reid Streets, and while he was still editor of the *Courier*, that the mind of WILLIAM BUCHANAN CARLISLE became overshadowed, and soon afterwards, irretrievably lost. The editorial department of the paper was not permitted to suffer, however, as that early and tried friend of the establishment, Colonel AUGUSTUS OLIVER ANDREWS, together with the Reverend URBAN SINKLER BIRD, were engaged in its support.

A. O. ANDREWS was born in Charleston. His education, collegiate, was thorough. Reared as a merchant, he has since become most prominent and useful. He has for many years been closely identified with the commercial interests of his native city. A long and distinguished administration as President of the Charleston Chamber of Commerce, is associated with his name. Fond of literature, his friendly and very intimate relations with the editors of the *Courier*, dating as they do from early life, gave him scope in the indulgence of a logical and facile pen. His diction is admirable; admitting of no addition or subtraction without risking the destruction of a charm. His writings—generally miscellaneous—admit of no substitution of terms. They have that *curiosa felicitas* which proves that in their preparation much thought and time have been judiciously expended. That portion of the *Courier* which is devoted to " Leisure moments with new publications," receives the attention of this discriminating writer.

Mr. BIRD, whose writings were miscellaneous and easy, became connected with the *Courier* in November, 1858. In February, 1865, he terminated his connection with the paper, and associated himself with the Reverend F. A. MOOD, and together, published, for a short time, *The Weekly Record*. Mr. BIRD went afterwards, to reside in Florida.

The second day after the occupation of Charleston by the forces of the United States, under Lieutenant-Colonel A. G. BENNETT, Commanding, and which occurred February 18th, 1865, the establishment of the *Courier* was taken possession of by STEWART L. WOODFORD, Lieutenant-Colonel of the 127th New York Volunteers, and Provost Marshal General. The seizure was under official orders from General QUINCY A. GILMORE, and is here appended :

"OFFICE PROVOST MARSHAL GENERAL, D. S., ⎱
       "CHARLESTON, S. C., February 20th, 1865. ⎰
" [*Special Orders No.* 1.]

" *The Charleston Courier* establishment is hereby taken "possession of, by the military authorities of the United "States. All the materials and property of said news-"paper, of every kind, will be immediately turned over "to Messrs. GEORGE WHITTEMORE and GEO. W. JOHNSON, "who are hereby authorized to issue a loyal Union news-"paper. They will receipt to Lieutenant-Colonel WOOD-"FORD, Provost Marshal General, D. S., for all property "taken possession of by them, under this order. They

"will keep possession of the building now used for that
"purpose.

    " By Command of Major-General Q. A. GILMORE.

                "STEWART L. WOODFORD,

        " Lieut. Colonel 127th N. Y. Volunteers,

             " Provost Marshal General, D. S."

It was announced officially, March 2d, 1865, that the
Military authorities had extended facilities to the editors
of the *Courier* for executing all kinds of Job Printing.
Mr. WILLIAM L. DAGGETT, who became connected with
the *Courier* as its foreman, in January, 1859—on the retirement of Mr. HENRY W. GWINNER, who had discharged
the duties with acceptance and laborious fidelity—was then
called as superintendent of Job Printing.

The new proprietors, made so by force of arms, suspended publication, April 5, 1865, and republished eight days
after, from 43 Hayne Street, two doors East from Meeting
Street. Both WHITTEMORE and JOHNSON were, up to the
time of their entrance into the City with the troops, attached to the Federal army, as correspondents of Northern
journals.

WILLIAM L. DAGGETT, who took charge of the Job department at the time mentioned, was born in New Bedford,
State of Massachusetts, August 6, 1824. After having
begun his apprenticeship, in 1832, with the late Colonel
SAMUEL GREEN, of the New London (Conn.) *Gazette*, he
worked in the office of the *Mercury*, a publication in the
Town of his nativity. He came to Charleston in 1838,
being then in his fourteenth year. After "sticking type"
in the offices of B. B. HUSSEY, BURGES & JAMES, *The
Charleston Mercury*, and *The Southern Patriot*, he was
called to the foremanship of *The Evening News*, in October, 1845, at the time that journal was started. Warmly

participating in the municipal contest of 1849, his energies were rewarded shortly after, by a civil appointment from the dominant party. In 1852, EDWARD C. COUNCELL and himself became co-partners, and as COUNCELL & DAGGETT were popular job printers. Withdrawing from that firm some time after he accepted the foremanship of *The Charleston Standard.* His next change found him in the office of the *Courier.* In his acceptance of the position he was called to, the proprietors were benefitted ; for, up to the present period, he has proved himself the most efficient, energetic and skillful of foremen.

Messrs. GEORGE WHITTEMORE and GEORGE W. JOHNSON continued to control the paper until the 24th of April, 1865, when Mr. JOHNSON, not only suddenly, but rather mysteriously, left the City. The paper was then issued by GEORGE WHITTEMORE & Co. It was then increased to full size from half a sheet; the dimensions being 16 by 11½ inches. The subscription price of $20 per annum, remained unchanged, and was paid in Federal currency. This condition of things remained until 20th November, 1865, when the firm of A. S. WILLINGTON & Co. again assumed control of the paper. It was then enlarged, and the subscription reduced to the ante-bellum rate of $10. In May, 1866, Mr. GEORGE WHITTEMORE left Charleston for New York. It is needless here, to state how the paper reverted to those who had for so many years upheld its ever popular usefulness and integrity. But a few weeks before this change, the office was, in consequence of a fire, which burned out the establishment, on the morning of 18th October, 1865, removed back to 111 East Bay, and once more occupied its old stand.

CHAPTER XIII.

THE COURIER AND ITS PRINCIPAL EDITORS—A. S. WILLING-
TON, R. YEADON, W. S. KING, AND OTHERS—NULLIFICA-
TION, A CIVIL EXCITEMENT, 1831–'32—THE COURIER
AND POLITICS—NEW YORK AND CHARLESTON LINE OF
STEAMERS—MEXICAN WAR—PONY EXPRESS—ELECTRO-
MAGNETIC TELEGRAPH.

THE *Courier* includes among its leading editors, within
the author's recollection, one of its founders, AARON SMITH
WILLINGTON. Mr. WILLINGTON became from practice,
a very excellent writer, of unaffected style and manner,
never attempting ambitious flights, always maintaining the
proper level of the subject he undertook to discuss. A
literary friend remarked in company, not a great while
ago, that Mr. WILLINGTON's excellent biographical sketch
of WILLIAM CRAFTS, at one time editor of the *Courier*,
would do credit to any journalist. Mr. WILLINGTON was
a man of wonderful energy, and nothing can more fully
demonstrate the fact, than his surmounting of difficulties
in early life, as publisher. His tour in Europe in 1851,
gave him a place in our native literature, through the instrumentality of an exceedingly well written volume, entitled, "A summer's tour in Europe, in 1851." A stroke
of apoplexy, sudden in its effect, which occurred on the
night of the 1st February, 1862, first indicated the approach of death; four hours later, on the morning of the
2nd, this highly esteemed editor and associate proprietor

of the *Courier*, closed his long, useful, and well directed life, within forty days of his 81st year. His remains were deposited in the cemetery of St. Philips' Church. The widow of Mr. WILLINGTON is now the representative of his interest in the paper.

RICHARD YEADON, who was the second associate proprietor of the *Courier*, was the only son of Col. RICHARD YEADON. He was born in this City, October 22, 1802. Mr. YEADON became the *de facto* editor of the *Courier*, July 1, 1832, taking the editorial pen, to wage the war of the Constitution, against nullification, as advanced by the State Rights Party. He took active charge of the editorial department of the paper, at the time of his connection with it as a partner, on the 1st January, 1833.

About this time, the *Courier*, which had pursued a commercial course, gradually became involved in politics; its tendency in this direction increased, and was, finally, more decided; in fact, it was hardly possible to escape the apparent vortex. It was the period of the great struggle of the Union, and the Nullification Parties, and no organ, not even one of the commercial and miscellaneous nature of the *Courier*, was suffered to retain a position of perfect neutrality. A position indeed of that sort would have been untenable by any journal in the presence of questions so vital!

The doctrine of nullification has been alluded to in connection with the press. This powerful fulcrum of public opinion, tended much to irritate that burning civil excitement; therefore, an outline of the contest cannot be regarded as out of place in this work.

Those who figured at the time, when there were daily apprehensions of the shedding of a brother's blood, are rapidly passing away. While complying with the behests of nature, they have, thus far, failed to leave to posterity, except in irregular form, any record of the most bitter of political disputations—one which has been such a prolific source of injury, politically, commercially, and socially.

It can be said of nullification, that though the question began to be agitated in the year 1824, it did not assume a very threatening shape until the celebrated protest of the South Carolina Legisture, on the subject of the tariff; a document of great historical interest, which was put forth in December, 1827. Mr. CALHOUN, regarded as the great High Priest of nullification, published about this time an exposition of the nullification doctrine.*

On the 4th July, 1831, General ROBERT Y. HAYNE, and others, addressed the nullifiers, and Colonel WILLIAM DRAYTON, the same day, in an oration which occupied over two hours of time, addressed the Union Party. Colonel DRAYTON was followed by THOS. R. MITCHELL, Judge HUGÉR, Judge LEE, HUGH S. LEGARÉ, JAMES L. PETIGRU, and others. From that period, party lines were formally drawn.

The General Assembly of South Carolina, on the 23d November, 1832, called a Convention. The Convention, with Governor HAMILTON at its head, passed, by a vote of

---

* Nullification was a word never used by John C. Calhoun. It was a term used by Thomas Jefferson. A venerable statesman and townsman of ours— he, who made the call in our State Legislature, in 1831, for a Convention—has furnished the author with the following extract of a letter, in justification of the assertion, to many unknown. The letter from which these sentences are taken, is dated June 9, 1865. The letter was written by a relative, a confidential friend in fact, of John C. Calhoun. In the following language the eminent statesman has spoken:

"Nullification is not my word. I never use it. I always say STATE INTERPOSITION. My purpose is a suspensive veto, to compell the installing of the highest tribunal provided by the Constitution, to decide on the point in dispute. I do not wish to destroy the Union. I only wish to make it honest. The Union is too strong to break. Nothing can break it, but the slavery question, if that can. If a Convention of the States were called, and it should decide that the protective policy is constitutional, what then? Then give it up."

136 to 27, the Ordinance of Nullification. This instrument ignored certain acts of Congress, laying duties on foreign commodities.

A proclamation, denunciatory of this Ordinance was made by President ANDREW JACKSON, dated at Washington, December 10, 1832. It was a powerful composition, four columns in length, and couched in language not to be mistaken. This proclamation, repugnant as it was to the nullifiers, gave hopes and assurances to those of the Union Party.

The nullifiers were for putting down the tariff, by the action of one State, with the expectation of being joined by the other Southern States. The Union and State Rights Party, were likewise opposed to the tariff, but advocated a Convention of the Southern States. They hoped by peaceful means to pursuade their tariff brethren to gradually lesson the burthens under which they labored. It could not be accomplished. Parties *pro* and *con*, already formed, increased numerically, civil strife waxed warm, and mischief—incalculable mischief was threatened. A sovereign State had openly defied, and by legislative enactment, annulled the laws of the Union. The silver cord so oft confessed, was about to be severed, and no man could then say at what hour the troubles were destined to burst in an overwhelming deluge of ruin and disaster.

With no intention to narrate the many incidents which were enacted during a period when the result of one single rash act could not have been foreseen, the author continues, and briefly narrates the settlement of that serious domestic dissonance.

Upon the enactment of Mr. CLAY'S tariff or compromise. bill, in February. 1833, which was a substitute for that of Mr. VERPLANK'S, nullification began to wane. The enactment of Mr. CLAY'S bill, together with the cogent influences

produced by BENJAMIN WATKINS LEIGH, who came as
Commissioner from Virginia to South Carolina, to promote
an adjustment between a sister State and the General Government, brought about a revocation of the Nullification
Ordinance, on the 15th March, 1833.   That obstacle having been removed, there was inaugurated a restoration to
harmony in our State.   Then came that era of good feeling
which was again to unite all in the bonds of social, if not
political brotherhood.   Alienated affections gradually returned to their wonted, but long deserted channels.   The
rankling wounds of the social, and even the family circle,
began to experience the healing influences, and all felt that
if party warfare had again to be waged, it should be characterized by the courtesies and charities of life.

A review of the troops by Governor HAYNE, HAMIL-
TON's successor, and a salute of one hundred guns, which
was fired on the 1st April, 1833, bespoke the end of nullification.   Thus it was, that the Union was saved, by the
spirit of concession and compromise, that presided at its
formation.

"Nothing in the nature of newspaper controversy" said
The Courier and Enquirer, of New York, during that exciting time, " could be more pointed, or more pungent, than
" the weapons of warfare wielded by *The Charleston Courier*,
" in doing battle with the CALHOUN cohorts in South Car-
" olina.   It is almost painful to stand by, and see the *exe-*
" *cution* done by the grape and cannister, which the *Cou-*
" *rier* throws into the nullification ranks.   Its shots tell,
" with fearful effect, upon the *Mercury* in particular."

The *Courier*, which is more of a commercial and miscellaneous than a political journal, has nevertheless played its
part, and that boldly in the issues which have, at different
periods, agitated the country.   In the era of nullification,
it was the leading Union organ in the State, and upheld

the Union cause against what it regarded an unconstitutional resistance to the laws of the Union within the
Union.   It upheld the cause of the Union, in the secession
crisis of 1851 and 1852, and threw its influence in favor
of co-operation against the secession element, as a choice of
evils.   Again, in 1860, during the secession era, it held the
election of a sectional President, on grounds of political
and practical hostility to the constitutional rights, and
cherished domestic institutions of the South, to be properly
and inevitably the knell of the Union, and went with the
State, and the South, in dissolving a connection with faith-
less confederates.

It is only, however, when such trials become inevitable,
that the proprietors of journals like the *Courier*, should
countenance a deviation from tenets, akin to those which
that journal has long adhered to, with determined persistency.

The unavoidable change of policy, alluded to in the editorship of the *Courier*, was greatly regretted by the associate proprietors.

Mr. YEADON continued to conduct the editorial department of the paper, until the strife of local, State and National politics was safely over, and society had once more
returned to a condition of repose.   Mr. YEADON withdrew
from the editorial chair, on the 4th November, 1844, in a
valedictory of three columns, addressed " To the Patrons of
the *Courier* and the Public."   Then it was, that he concen-
trated his labors upon his exacting profession—the law.
The enticement of composition, however, upon all topics of
public interest, natural to one of his remarkable intellectual endowment, he could not resist, and, at intervals he
contributed to the columns of his paper.

With that stern and inflexible disposition, evinced by
him when assailed, he responded to the gross and vulgar

attack of *The New York Herald*, when the latent hostility of that journal was aroused against himself and his paper, in January, 1858. The reply was not only curt, but convincing. Here is the article: "The New York Herald.— " This scurrilous journal has made a gross, vulgar, and un- " provoked attack on one of the editors of the *Courier*, so " utterly at war with propriety and decency, as to require " no other notice, than an expression of unmitigated con- " tempt for the author, whose notorious venality, destitu- " tion of moral sense, and insensibility to shame, have long " since caused him to be put to the social ban, and to be " *tabooed* by the press of New York, where he is generally " regarded as a moral leper, whose touch is pollution, and " whose disease is so deeply seated, that not Arbana and " Pharpar, rivers of Damascus, nor Jordan, and all the wa- " ters of Israel, can wash him clean." This rebuke was generally commented upon at the time, by the New York and Carolina presses.

In the capacity of editor, Mr. YEADON was recognized as a man of power ; of a vigor, in fact, equal to that which he exhibited as a lawyer. He wrote clearly, with a mind eminently logical, and a memory stored with facts, always ready with his authorities, and prompt in seizing the strong points of his argument. Quick and comprehensive in his intelligence, he was never otherwise than patient, and indefatigable in investigation. "And thus working, toiling " incessantly, day and night, now in his law office, or in " the courts, and now writing column after column for the " *Courier*, this strong man continued to labor, until the de- " cree went forth from the Supreme Governor of the world, " that his labors should cease." Sorrowing relatives and friends witnessed the closing of his grave, in the cemetery of the Circular Church, on the afternoon of the 26th of

12

April, 1870. He was 68 years of age, when his death occurred.

WILLIAM S. KING, the junior of that co-partnership which was formed in 1833, was born at Queenstown, in the western part of the State of New-York, 23d December, 1801. He had been for about twelve years, the manager of the business, mercantile, and miscellaneous departments, when he succeeded, after the withdrawal of Mr. YEADON, to the editorial chair of the *Courier*. This paper had, even then, become a prominent and popular reflex of public opinion.

Mr. KING was distinguished for cool judgment, general intelligence, and for his indisputable authority among the craft. His whole course of procedure, for thirty-seven years, while in the several departments which he occupied, will bear ample testimony to his natural gifts and capacities, while at the same time, they will give equal proof of his general amenity; his reluctance to give pain; his dislike of strife, and all unnecessary discussion.

From the 1st January, 1833, when he became part proprietor in the *Courier*, he devoted himself to the management of its commercial and business departments. In these employments it will be admitted, that he displayed that zeal and energy which placed him in the front-rank of his profession. He was of a social and genial disposition; a quality, indispensably necessary to men living in this sphere of society. We need scarcely say here, that it was the high appreciation of his many qualities of worth, which moved the members of the "Charleston Typographical Society" so repeatedly to call him to preside over their Society, an old association of printers, and of which body, JAMES GRANT was the father, and founder.

It was during the administration of Mr. KING, as editor

and manager, that the first line of steamships was established between New York and Charleston. The persistency evinced by Captain MICHAEL BERRY, aided by the *Courier's* unceasing importunings, went very far in the accomplishment of this important enterprise.

The breaking out of the Mexican war, at the close of 1846, offered a fine field for newspaper enterprise in the South. The time then expended in the transmission of the regular mail between New Orleans and New York, was seven days. To obtain advices of the struggle then about to begin in that distracted country, in advance of the mail facilities, became the fixed purpose of the management of the *Courier*, and MOSES Y. BEACH, of the New York *Sun*. The telegraph line then extended only as far as Richmond, Virginia. In this attempt to out-strip government, Mr. BEACH very readily obtained the co-operation of Mr. KING, and a "Pony Express" was conjointly established. It went at once into effect, and the first intelligence from the land of the Montezumas, was received and published in this City, exclusively, the 27th March, 1847. Thousands of extras were gratuitously distributed, from the office of the *Courier*, to an eager crowd, full twenty-four hours in advance of the United States Mail. The running of this express, by which the intelligence was received and published exclusively in this paper, while the war lasted, was of immense pecuniary benefit to the proprietors.

The point at which the regular mail was out-stripped, was between Mobile and Montgomery, where one hundred and fifty miles of staging had to be performed, consuming thirty-six hours of time. This ground was, by a contract made with J. C. RIDDLE, to be covered within twelve hours, and to overtake the previous day's mail; the riders of the express taking with them not less than three nor more than five pounds of mail matter. In this great un-

dertaking, $750 was paid for each successful trip. A fail-
ure very rarely occurred. Several horses were killed, and
only in one instance was the life of a rider sacrificed to the
accomplishment of an adventure quite hazardous, the *modus operandi* of which, has never been revealed. This was
the first step actually taken which led to the formation of
the now famous " News Association."

Mr. KING was the first, and most prominent of our
Southern editors, whose zealous pen contributed so extensively to the support of the " Electro Magnetic Telegraph,"
which has accomplished so much in revolutionizing the
newspaper business. The limit of its usefulness to the
press has, however, not yet been reached. This want was
supplied to Charleston, in April, 1847. The leaders of the
Courier incessantly plead in behalf of this momentous
subject, whereby Charleston, like other commercial empo-
riums of the republic, soon received and transmitted mercantile, military, political and general intelligence, with
the speed of lightning. Communication with Columbia,
by this method was opened under the management of G. L.
HUNTINGTON, of the Charleston office, and Dr. L. C. DUN-
CAN, of the Columbia office, at twenty minutes past four
o'clock, on the afternoon of December 1st, 1847, from the
building formerly owned by the " Union Insurance Company," on State Street, near Broad Street. The very first
message sent was : " Columbia—Do you get my writing ?"
" Charleston—I get all you write to me." The Hon. WM.
D. PORTER, a member of the General Assembly, then in
session in Columbia, received from Major ALEXANDER
BLACK, a Director, the first regular or business message.
It was an inquiry as to whether a memorial and charter
for the Telegraph Company had been received. The first
dispatch to the press, was received by the *Courier*, Mr.
KING being also a Director. It was dated at Columbia,

at 8 o'clock, P. M. The first Telegraph line contracted for in the United States, the reader may like to know, was put in operation, in June, 1844, between Washington and Baltimore.

These comments on the career of a practical man like Mr. KING, should encourage all young men of the craft. In him can be seen a modest artisan coming to a strange land, at the age of twenty years, accepting position as a journeyman compositor, growing in public opinion, prosperous in fortune, and gathering in a short space of time a host of friends about him. How was it that under these circumstances he achieved so much? By processes which are open to the youngest and humblest follower of the art, chief among which is attention to business, with a constant consideration of the duty which lay before him. Society here has, generally, ranked Mr. KING, as a model journalist. He is, therefore, one, whose course and conduct ought to be studied and imitated.

It will suffice to close this tribute from the frank and generous testimonial of JOHN MILTON CLAPP, of the *Mercury*, who terminated his very feeling eulogium with the following compliment: " That in his long association with " him of fifteen years, as neighbor and *confrère* in the edi- " torial world, he could recall no word, or act of Colonel " KING, which has need to be forgiven." Does not this go far to verify the assertion made by the author of this humble sketch, that with the newspaper press of Charleston, there once existed a grateful and happy social organization.

CHAPTER XIV.

AT the death of Mr. KING, which occurred March 19,
1852, the editorial duties devolved upon his assistant, AL-
EXANDER CARROLL, the business management upon WM.
LAIDLER, and that of finance upon JAMES H. MURRELL.

ALEXANDER CARROLL was born in Cheltenham, England, and before his arrival in Charleston, was associated
with the London press. He came to his adopted home in
August, 1849, and through the instrumentality of Mr.
KING, became, for a while, an *attaché* of the *Mercury;*
subsequently, through the same influence, aided by Mr.
JOHN HEART, he was, before the close of the year, called
to the direction of the *State Rights Republican*, then published in Columbia, South Carolina, by I. C. MORGAN ; W.
B. CARLISLE, the editor, having withdrawn with the view
of associating himself with EDWIN DE LEON, in the publication of *The Telegraph*. Mr. CARROLL was called to the
editorial staff of the *Courier* early in 1851, by Mr. KING,
who desired respite from duties, which were most arduous.

In Mr. CARROLL were combined great energy, close application and versatility of intellect; qualities though indispensable, not often met with, in an editor. His power

of endurance, also, was marvellous. Mr. CARROLL continued a faithful worker, up to the time of his illness, and death. The latter event took place August 21, 1856, just seven years after his arrival in Charleston. His remains were interred in the cemetery of St. John's Lutheran Church.

WILLIAM LAIDLER, who became one of the proprietors of the *Courier*, January 1st, 1854, is a son of Captain WM. LAIDLER, an old ship master of Charleston. Mr. LAIDLER, (brother-in-law of the late Colonel KING,) was born in this City, July 30, 1812. A thorough craftsman, he began his apprenticeship in the office of *The City Gazette and Daily Advertiser*, under JAMES HAIG, on the 9th June, 1825. He was transferred to the *Courier*, at the instance of Mr. WILLINGTON, in the summer of 1828, and while in the employment of that journal, in the fall of 1833, the guardians of his covenant of apprenticeship returned his " indenture" to him with honor, and expressions of satisfaction for having been so faithful in the performance of his duty.

JAMES H. MURRELL, whose association with the *Courier* bears date, March 13, 1841, was born in Stateburg, South Carolina, on the " High Hills of Santee," May 12, 1814. His education was academic, and under the tutorship of the Reverend JESSE HARTWELL and Doctor RICHARD BAKER. He was, subsequently, prepared for West Point, by WILLIAM CAPERS, nephew of Bishop CAPERS. When about to leave for West Point, that institution of education became the scene of insubordination. A relative and a neighbor of Mr. MURRELL, being prominent in that tumultuary disturbance, it was deemed advisable to change the provision of life thus cut out for him. After having finished a course of commercial studies, first in Camden, and afterwards in Columbia, he came to Charleston.

Mr. LAIDLER and Mr. MURRELL, are so well known, that it is not necessary to point to the earnest devotion to business displayed by the former, upon whom devolves the general management of the establishment. Still less, need the systematic, courteous, efficient and satisfactory manner in which the latter has administered his department be alluded to. For a period of not less than eleven years, Mr. MURRELL has had as his assistant, Mr. S. H. KING, one of the ablest of accountants, and third son of the late WM. S. KING.

HENRY M. CUSHMAN, the successor of Mr. CARROLL, in the editorship of the *Courier*, was from New Haven, Connecticut. He was called from the position of editor of *The Daily Times*, of Boston, Massachusetts, in December, 1856. He was thoroughly educated, a clever writer, a skillful selector and compiler of news, and well acquainted with the duties of a newspaper office. His course, as a journalist in the South, was brief. He died April 13, 1857, and was buried at Magnolia Cemetery.

It was after the death of Mr. CUSHMAN that JAMES L. HATCH left the *Standard*, and connected himself with the editorial department of the *Courier*. This editor will be noticed more at length elsewhere, in connection with the *Standard*.

WILLIAM BUCHANAN CARLISLE, who possessed rare abilities as a writer, and was one of the most profound of mathematicians, was in turn, and to the period of his affliction, the very competent editor-in-chief.

In August, 1857, JOSEPHUS WOODRUFF, became connected with the *Courier* as Phonographic Reporter. Mr. WOODRUFF may justly be regarded as the first " Local Reporter" known to the Charleston press. He had previously been employed as mailing clerk, at the office of the *Mercury ;* while there he began the study of phonography or short-hand writing, by the aid of PITMAN's Manual, a copy having been sent to that office for review and notice. Notwithstanding repeated failures in his early reports he steadily persevered in the study of the art, and has since acquired considerable reputation as an expert reporter. He was correspondent and reporter for the *Courier*, of the proceedings of the General Assembly, in 1860, which passed the act providing for the Secession Convention; assisted in the extended reports of the Democratic National Convention of South Carolina, which split at Charleston; was almost the sole reporter for the *Courier* during the war, and reported the proceedings of the Reconstruction Convention of 1868. His connection with the paper continued up to July, 1868, at which time he was elected clerk of the Senate of South Carolina.

The winter of 1860, found Mr. HENRY SPARNICK, an under graduate at the College of Charleston, in the service of the *Courier*, as a special correspondent, at the State Capitol. Upon the assembling of the Provisional Congress of the Confederated States, at Montgomery, Alabama, he went thither in the same capacity. When the seat of Government was removed to Richmond, Virginia, Mr. SPARNICK followed it there, continuing his duties as correspondent, until the civil service of the Government compelled him to relinquish his association with the press. In July, 1865, he accepted position as "City Reporter" of the *Courier*. Mr. WOODRUFF's phonographic ability calling him to another department of the paper. In that capacity Mr. SPARNICK remained until 1867, when he, by promotion, became assistant editor, which place he filled until the close of the presidential campaign of 1868. A change in his political convictions made his continuance with the *Courier* incompatible with the interests of that journal, and he resigned.

Colonel THOMAS YOUNG SIMONS, the present editor-in-chief of the *Courier*, and who was called to that station in October, 1865, was born within distinct sound of St. Michael's tuneful bells, October 1, 1828. While passing to a consideration of his most promising career, the author will remark, that his youth gave promise of that mental capacity, which has been so advantageously developed, in more mature years. After a successful preparatory course of studies at the Charleston College, he is next found treading the classic ground of "Yale;" there, he graduated in August, 1847. On his return to Charleston, he became, in 1848, assistant teacher in the Charleston High School, and continued until near the close of 1849 ; was admitted to the bar in February, 1850, having studied law with his kinsman, General JAMES SIMONS; was elected to the Legislature, in October, 1854, and served his constituents, faithfully, until the autumn of 1858, when he was returned by his constituency to that body, as Chairman of the Charleston delegation, and served until 1860. He retired from the Legislature, and was elected a member of the Convention, called by the free choice of the people of South Carolina, and which withdrew the State from the Federal Union, December 20, 1860. While the State was preparing for war, Colonel SIMONS raised two companies; was elected, and served, as Captain of one of them—the Charleston Light Infantry, afterwards company " B," 27th (Gaillard's) Regiment, until the memorable surrender, April 13, 1865. Without relinquishing the weightier matters of the law, Colonel SIMONS entered the ranks of professional journalists, bringing to the chair of editorship, a full appreciation of the requirements, the dignity, and responsibility of the profession.

In July, 1867, Mr. JOHN A. MOROSO, succeeded Mr. SPARNICK, as "City Reporter." Mr. MOROSO is a graduate of the Charleston College, and received the degree of Bachelor of Arts, in March, 1866, and subsequently, the degree of Master of Arts, in 1869. He was admitted to the bar, in April, 1867. Mr. MOROSO remained the "Local" of the *Courier* up to July, 1869. During the canvass of that year, he was the traveling correspondent of this journal, accompanying the nominees of the "Reform Party" during their exciting and arduous tour. His letters were written with vigor and piquancy. On his return, in October, 1869, he was placed in the chair of the news editor of the *Courier*, which had been briefly occupied by Mr. P. J. MALONE. This position he continues to hold.

The chair of "City Reporter," made vacant by the advancement of Mr. MOROSO, in the summer of 1869, was soon occupied by Mr. F. W. MILLER. This gentleman was, at one time, engaged with the late S. LE ROY HAMMOND, in the publication of *The Port Folio*, a sprightly weekly of considerable merit. His pen at various times, before and since the suspension of that paper, has contributed to the City journals. In the exacting vocation in which he now labors, requiring as it does, probity and capacity, Mr. MILLER is well qualified by long service, and varied experience, no less than by natural ability and industry.

The *Courier* is indebted in no small degree for its character as an enlightened chronicler of transpiring events, to its intelligent corps of correspondents, both foreign and domestic. We may mention as prominent among those who have been regarded as regular contributors from abroad, Mr. WILLIAM YOUNG, as "O. P. Q.," and WM. HENRY RUSSELL, and also Dr. C. S. KING, who, up to the summer of 1853, wrote from Paris, and who so graphically described the secret journey of himself and his compatriots—Doctors TURNIPSEED, HENRY, HOLT, and DRAPER—from the latter place, through Brussels, Vienna, Jassy, Odessa, Kichenew, to Simpheropol, and the stirring scenes enacted during the Crimean war, around the then Gibraltar of Russia—Sebastopol. There are the names, also, of Dr. JOHN D. BRUNS, Dr. F. PEYRE PORCHER, RUDOLPH SIEGLING, and J. J. FICKEN, who, as tourists, corresponding for the paper, have made us as familiar with what they have seen, as if we had seen for ourselves.

Of the domestic correspondents, there have been many. Most frequent among them have been "Sumter," (GEO. W. OLNEY, jr.) "Pink," the first, (J. W. KENNEDY) "D. I. O.," and "Pink," the second, (L. ISRAELS) who have written from New York; "Blue," among others, from New Orleans; "M. P.," (Miss PENINA MOISE,) whose graceful literary productions, in prose and verse, from without and within the city, have been welcomed for many years; "Juhl," (J. J. FLEMING) of Sumter, and "Leo," (E. KINGMAN,) who is authority at the seat of Government, and whose admirable letters, for a period of about thirty years, have never been without interest.

It was with a keen sense of loss, that the *Courier*, on the morning of 16th February, 1870, thus addressed itself to the task of recording the death of WILLIAM ROGERS:

"This gentleman, so long known to the *habitués* of the "*Courier* office, by his unremitting devotion to the duties "of the department in which, for more than a third of a "century, he had moved and had his being, passed away "from all earth's cares at yesterday's dawn."

"The recollections of him, by many, will go back to his "first connection with the interests of the *Courier*, as su-"perintendent of the Merchants' Exchange and Reading "Room, under the proprietorship, of his warm friend, the "late Colonel WM. S. KING. Protracted and painful ill-"ness, for several months, laid its iron hand upon him, and

13

" at last unwillingly compelled him to withdraw from the
" discharge of duties to which he had applied himself, so
" unweariedly, so long, and so faithfully. He will be
" missed by numbers—he was so well known to all—but
" by none more than by the commercial community, who
" rightly estimated the conscientiousness and rectitude,
" which he ever displayed, throughout his long career, as a
" statistician and reporter in the ' Prices Current and Mar-
" ket' bureau of this journal. In the reputation and au-
" thority which the *Courier* has earned in this department,
" he felt a just pride ; and it was in him a labor of love, to
" guard and strengthen the standard which had been at-
" tained. In the important change of cotton statistics, his
" trust-worthiness and experience were valued abroad, as
" well as at home, and the occasions of a recognition there-
" of, were not infrequent."

" He had passed his 64th year, thirty-seven of which
" had been spent in the service of this journal. From the
" editorial *sanctum*, to the youngest *attaché* of the *Cou-*
" *rier*—all feel sad, that the kindly greetings of the plea-
" sant old gentleman, will salute them no more—forever."

CHAPTER XV.

THE *Charleston Mercury*, a daily morning print, which
was established as a literary journal, on the 1st January,
1822, by that classic scholar, EDMUND MORFORD, who had
then returned to Charleston, was purchased and converted
into a political organ by HENRY LAURENS PINCKNEY, June
1, 1823. From that date it became the representative of
the Free Trade and State Rights Party, of South Carolina. In the warfare of parties, State and National, Mr.
PINCKNEY was excelled by few, as a political editor.
Who of us that knew him, can fail to recollect the marked
bearing of the accomplished editor, and astute statesman?

From the time that Mr. PINCKNEY became proprietor
of *The Charleston Mercury*, the editorial management of
the paper was assumed by him. Mr. MORFORD did not
withdraw, but remained an editorial *attaché* of the paper,
until shortly before his death, which occurred in New Jersey, February 4, 1833, (age 51 years.) The *Mercury* became JEFFERSON Republican in principle, yet liberal in its
tone. The firmness and tenacity with which Mr. PINCK-
NEY—who combined, in more than an ordinary degree, the

qualities of writer and speaker—maintained his own views, were always mingled with a spirit of conciliation and tolerance for the opinions of others. Mr. PINCKNEY was, on the 31st October, 1832, succeeded by JOHN A. STUART, former editor of *The Evening Post*, to whom Mr. PINCKNEY had transferred the paper.

Mr. PINCKNEY was born in Charleston, September 24, 1794; graduated at the South Carolina College, in 1812; sent by his constituents to the Legislature at an early age, and became speaker of the House of Representatives, in 1831; was elected Intendant of the City of Charleston, September 3, 1832, during the nullification excitement, which, as previously mentioned, began in the summer of 1831. In this election, nullification boasted of a hard fought victory. The duel between two well known citizens, GEORGE ROBERTSON and THEODORE GAILLARD, grew out of it. In 1833, Mr. PINCKNEY was elected to Congress from Charleston District without opposition; re-elected in 1835, and was Mayor of Charleston, in 1839. He was installed as Collector of the Port of Charleston, 1st August, 1840. At a subsequent period, January, 1845, he was elected Tax Collector, for the Parishes of St. Philip and St. Michael.

Mr. PINCKNEY was a strong Southern writer; the author of "Memoirs of Doctor JONATHAN MAXEY," who was by the unanimous request of the Trustees, made the first President of the South Carolina College, when that institution was established, in 1804. He also wrote the "Memoirs of ROBERT Y. HAYNE," and the "Life and public services of ANDREW JACKSON." Few names have stood more conspicuous in our country, than that of PINCKNEY, whether we consider the services they have rendered in the cabinet, or in the field. Mr. PINCKNEY died February 3, 1863.

The year that the *Mercury* came into existence, was fertile in newspapers; for besides that which has since been known as the leading organ of the Free Trade and State Rights Party, there were *The Evening Spy*, a weekly, and *The Southern Intelligencer*, a daily. It would seem, that "the reapers multiplied, but the harvest did not abound."

Allusion having been made to the extreme cold weather of January, 1737, in the second chapter of this work, reminds us of an equally cold snap, which prevailed in February, 1835, and the particulars of which are to be found in the columns of that once faithful custodian of State Rights doctrine, the *Mercury*. Many of the present residents of Charleston remember the sufferings endured on the 7th and 8th of February of that year. Up to the night of the 6th of that month, the weather was comfortable; but at a more advanced period of the night, a change took place. This change was accompanied with occasional but heavy showers of sleet, with a growing blast from the northwest, which continued until Saturday morning. At 10 o'clock on the night of Saturday, the thermometer—one which was suspended about nineteen feet from the ground, and which faced West—stood at 14 degrees above zero; at 7 o'clock Sunday morning, it was 2 degrees above zero, and from 7 A. M. until 12 M., it remained at 18 degrees above zero.

Wine and porter, in bottles, in the Southern parts of houses, assumed a solid form, and the salt water in the docks and adjacent mill-ponds was frozen. It was in this winter that the orange trees, along the coasts of South Carolina, Georgia, and Florida were killed.

From the richly freighted columns of the same journal, which, figuratively speaking, was the main support of the commonwealth in its brightest day, we take the following incident, which was an exhibition of popular feeling, that took place in Charleston, August 21, 1835:

Summary punishment was, that day, inflicted upon an individual named RICHARD WOOD, who for a number of years, had been carrying on at his shop in Queen Street, near East Bay, the business of a barber, and purchaser of stolen goods from negroes, under the assumed name of W R. CARROLL.

On the day mentioned, a number of citizens, prominent among whom was JOHN LYDE WILSON, assembled at an early hour. Three or four of the number congregated, were deputed to enter WOOD'S shop and bring him forth. This was executed with the utmost promptness and decision, and without the least disturbance, although it had been given out that certain death would be the doom of the first who made the attempt. WOOD was immediately marched down to Price's Wharf, (now Accommodation Wharf,) tied to a post, and there received about twenty lashes upon his bare back; a tub of tar was then emptied upon his head, in such a manner as to cause it to extend over his whole body, and the miscreant individual was decorated with a covering of loose cotton, the principal material in which he had carried on his illicit traffic, with much advantage to his purse. After this operation had been quietly performed, he was escorted by a large number of persons through the market, and the most public streets of the City, in order that others, guilty of the like practice, should take warning by his fate. He was then lodged in jail, to prevent his being exposed to further personal injury.

This spoiler of the public, had been, for a length of time, carrying on his dishonest traffic in defiance of the community, and it became the fixed determination of the inhabitants of Charleston no longer to submit, quietly, to such a system of spoliation and robbery.

It is said that WOOD, alias CARROLL, from his barber shop, exported about sixty bales of cotton annually. Several trunks were taken therefrom, which contained silver spoons, fine linen, ladies' apparel complete, bed drapery, etc. From this digression we will return to the successor of Mr. PINCKNEY.

JOHN A. STUART, into whose hands the *Mercury* was resigned by Mr. PINCKNEY, at the time already named, was a graduate of the South Carolina College. He brought to the sanctum of the *Mercury*, not only a well informed mind, but exquisite taste in literature; was as playful as he was reflective; was capable of satire, as well as analysis; with rapid transition "from grave to gay, from lively to severe." He scarcely suffered a single day's paper to go forth to his readers, without a display of sound judgment, flavored with keen and racy wit.

During the period in which Mr. STUART edited the *Mercury*, and towards the close of his editorial career, JOHN MILTON CLAPP was connected with the paper as associate editor, and for some months, owing to the impaired condition of Mr. STUART's health, it was under his sole conduct and management. Mr. STUART died at Beaufort, in this State, the place of his nativity, on the 3d May, 1853, in the 53d year of his age.

JOHN MILTON CLAPP, was from Pittsfield, Ohio, at which place he was born, in 1810. He was called by STUART in 1837, from Beaufort, South Carolina, where he then was, to the assistant editor's chair of the *Mercury*.

Mr. CLAPP was a writer of classical taste and culture; was capable of the most felicitous periods, and, like STUART, endowed with a keen appreciation of the humorous, displaying that quality, not only in private, but occasionally, also, to the public. Mr. CLAPP graduated at "Yale" when in his 21st year. He was one of the ablest of editors, and showed it in all the high conditions and exactions of editorial duties and emergencies. Had we the space, we could amply illustrate by examples, the truth and justice of the distinction which has been awarded to him. At one time he editorially conducted the *Southern Quarterly Review*, which became the repository of articles of interest to persons of widely different tastes and pursuits, and in the pages of that publication, the historian, the antiquary, the genealogist, the bibliographer and belles-letters scholar could always find something worthy of his attention.

A sad accident did much to shorten his days. About 2 o'clock, on the afternoon of the 22d September, 1852, he stepped on a balcony on the second floor of the *Mercury* office—then located where the First National Bank now is—when a portion of it gave way, precipitating him a distance of some eighteen or twenty feet, on a brick pavement, breaking his right leg, and otherwise injuring him. Mr. CLAPP died in this City, December 16, 1857. His remains now rest in the burial ground of the Charleston Typographical Society, at Magnolia.

The chair occupied by Mr. STUART for about fifteen years, was left to be filled by Colonel JOHN E. CAREW, who, on the 1st February, 1847, became editor and sole proprietor of that famous journal. This position Colonel CAREW sustained individually, with marked characteristic ability, adorning and illustrating that journal by profound erudition, classical lore, and the chastened elegance of his pen.

THOMAS A. HAYDEN was, about this time, the foreman and business manager of the *Mercury*. He was a native of Florida, and a printer by trade. In all the relations of life, his conduct was such as to command the respect and confidence of his fellow-citizens, and secured to him many warm friends. Mr. HAYDEN died at Rutherfordton, North

Carolina, November 21, 1851. He was succeeded by ADAM
C. CAVIS. CHARLES P. L. WESTENDORFF had charge of
the commercial department of the *Mercury*, for many years.

Not long prior to 1849, Mr. JOHN HEART—who was at
the head of *The Spectator* and *Young Hickory*, the organs
of the CALHOUN Democracy, in Washington, and which in
1842 killed off Mr. VAN BUREN—was called from that
City, and appointed to a position on the *Mercury;* subsequently became one of the editors, and on 1st September,
1849, was recognized as a joint proprietor. The firm was,
at that time, announced as CAREW & HEART. Colonel
CAREW retired from the *Mercury* on the 26th January,
1852, taking leave of his patrons, gracefully, feelingly, and
modestly—that trait so delicately described by ADDISON,
" which sets off every great talent which a man can be
possessed of." It was after the retirement of Colonel CA-
REW, that JOHN HEART and WILLIAM R. TABER, jr., under the firm of HEART & TABER, became the proprietors of
the *Mercury*.

JOHN HEART, was born in Philadelphia, Pennsylvania,
May 19, 1806. He had active practical habits, and also a
large experience of the workings of the press. Members
of the craft will recollect that he was once President of
the Charleston Typographical Society.

WILLIAM R. TABER, jr., was born in this City on the
18th April, 1828. He was a graceful, accomplished, versatile, and genial writer, and a good essayist. After four
years of editorship—short years to one so young and promising, a sudden and melancholy event occurred on the 29th
September, 1856, by which our City press lost, in the death
of Mr. TABER, a distinguished member of its fraternity;
the community a fine scholar, and society an amiable and
finished gentleman.

While in the zenith of his editorial career, he responded

to a call to the field of honor, in defence of a series of articles which received editorial sanction. The result of the
call was fatal to Mr. TABER. He fell at the third fire,
" mortally wounded in the upper part of the head," on
the Washington Race Course, the place selected for the
meeting, at half-past 4 o'clock, on the afternoon of the day
and year above mentioned, while vindicating the principles of the *Mercury's* motto, taken from OVID's Golden Age,
to wit: " *Vindice nullo sponte sua sine lege fides rectum-
que colentur.*" In the City journals of the 2d October,
1856, there can be found the correspondence relating to
the cause which had so fatal a termination.

Col. R. BARNWELL RHETT, jr., became the purchaser of
the interest of his kinsman, Mr. TABER, March 2, 1857.

On the 1st July, 1858, Mr. HEART sold his interest to
Colonel RHETT, and returned to Washington City. While
there he was made Superintendent of the Printing Bureau,
and was a successful manager of that large and intricate
concern. Mr. HEART subsequently—at the breaking out
of the war—resigned his position, and returned to the
South. Some years after, he removed to Memphis and
established a newspaper, called *The Commercial.* That
paper became a popular organ in Tennessee. Col. RHETT
has since become known as sole proprietor of the *Mercury.*

But once within the memory of the oldest inhabitant,
were the sportive citizens of Charleston favored with such
a treat as was enjoyed by them on the 17th December,
1851. From the *Mercury*, we learn that early on the
morning of that day, the thermometer indicated a degree
of cold which had not been experienced in this latitude for
at least sixteen years preceding At early morn the cloudy
canopy of heaven began dispensing a shower of snow,
which continued throughout the day, and up to a late hour
at night. Though the weather had not been such as to

freeze the earth, the streets, were, nevertheless, heavily coated with snow, and an opportunity was given several spirited individuals, among whom we recollect to have seen, Messrs. E. H. JACKSON, the brothers BUTTERFIELD, HUB-BARD, MOSES LEVY and others, glide through our streets with two improvised sleighs. The spectacle was quite creditable, and the novelty of sleigh-riding was for once witnessed in the streets of Charleston.

R. BARNWELL RHETT, jr., the last proprietor of the *Mercury*, proved himself a vigorous writer. As editor, he maintained the cause of State Rights and the South, with the same tenacity which had, for thirty years, marked the course of that journal. The cause which that editor so earnestly advocated, had an able and ardent advocate in his coadjutor—EDMUND RHETT, his younger brother. The columns of the *Mercury* will attest the boldness and vigor of the trenchant pen of this writer, and it was in support of the principles of that journal that he pre-eminently distinguished himself. "Almost before he was entitled to the *toga virilis*," writes a friend, "he took high rank among the thinkers of the period, and placed himself, side by side, with the strong men who were to fight the great battle, the result of which was to decide the future destiny of thirty millions of the human race."

In the summer of 1860, WM. A. COURTENAY was invited to take charge of the business department of the *Mercury*, and entered upon the duties on the 1st October, following. In the ensuing three months, he made a thorough and advantageous change in the business details of the office, and introduced into the establishment, one of HOE & Co's double cylinder presses, upon which the paper was printed up to the time its material was removed to Columbia. At the close of the following year he withdrew from the *Mercury*, and entered the army of the Confederate States. Captain

COURTENAY brought to the management of the *Mercury*, a well cultivated and active business mind, which still maintains, in other vocations, all its energies, with increased usefulness.

Yet another name is linked with the chain which connects the editorship of that paper. It is that of one of Carolina's poets—HENRY TIMROD. As editor, whether writing from the sanctum of *The South Carolinian*, published in Columbia, by the graceful and discursive writer, F. G. DE FONTAINE, the sedulous printer, JULIEN A. SELBY (the present proprietor of the Columbia *Phœnix*, whose comprehension of all the multifarious details which are met within his sisyphean task is well known) and himself, in the fourth year of the war, or from the " Local's" chair of the *Mercury*, his style was uniformly elegant. Is not his " Vision of Poesy" entitled to this distinction ?

The name of TIMROD will descend to posterity, unexcelled by any Southern Poet, as suggestive of chasteness, gentleness, and purity of style ; always graceful, imaginative and tender.

With pride and pleasure does the author mention, that he was one of Mr. TIMROD's earliest and most intimate acquaintances, and that the Poet, from his youth to manhood, and up to the period of his death, regarded him as a friend in whom he could, and did confide the innermost workings of one of the most sensitive of hearts. The career of this genius—genius gushing with tender and holy emotions, was too soon closed. He died in Columbia, on the 8th October, 1867. He went to his rest

> " Like a bright exhalation in the Evening,
> And no man saw him more."

These were the men who stood prominently before the public, as the master minds of that renowned political journal—that brilliant advocate of the pure government of the fathers, in defence of which it showed a vigor and genius which made it peerless in its day. It is a subject of regret, even with the many of those who differed, *toto cœlo*, from the political doctrines of the *Mercury*, that it should, at last, have been forced to succumb with the thousands of fallen fortunes of our City. It was the ruthless torch of Major-General SHERMAN'S legions which forced the suspension of the *Mercury*, in February, 1865. Its material being in Columbia, at the time that band of vandals visited it, fell a prey to the devouring torch applied to the beautiful capital of the State; an act which the genius of history should blush while blotting her pages with its record, and which will ever remain a stain upon the military escutcheon of its destroyer.

Colonel RHETT resumed the publication of the *Mercury*, November 19, 1866. During the last two years of its existence, ending in November of 1868, its associate editors were F. W. DAWSON, ROSWELL T. LOGAN, R. M. FULLER, and Doctor H. BAER. The general abilities of the *Mercury*, irrespective of its politics, always made it a popular favorite.

14

CHAPTER XVI.

THE *Southern Standard* was another morning paper. It had daily, tri-weekly and weekly editions, and was the successor of *The Sun;* in fact, was first published with the material which was purchased from the proprietors of that paper. It was founded by Messrs. B. C. PRESSLEY, KER BOYCE and M. C. MORDECAI. " Perseverance keeps honor bright," was its motto. The *Standard* came into existence, on the 1st July, 1851, under the editorship of B. C. PRESSLEY, assisted by W. C. RICHARDS, who was, for about five years, the editor of a periodical called *The Southern Literary Messenger*, and Dr. T. C. SKRINE, formerly editor of *The Sun*. A. G. MAGRATH and S. Y. TUPPER frequently wrote for this paper. The place of publication was then in the rear of the " Exchange."

The proprietors of *The Southern Standard* were induced, by the perils and necessities of the times, to establish in Charleston, an organ opposed to the agitating question of secession of South Carolina. The Resistance or Co-operation Party of the State was not divided as to her right to secede ; but many were convinced that such a movement at that time, would be fatal to the cause of resistance. It must have been with the greatest reluctance that the proprietors took the step during that political condition of the State, to widen that division, or do that which would make it thus apparent to the enemies of the principles which actuated the proprietors of the *Standard*. It was not free for the paper, it seemed, to choose in the matter. The issue came in such a form as made silence and self-respect wholly inconsistent with each other. It was asserted, in the face of the fact, that the State was pledged to secession, and that the supposed minority was bound to submit. And if, as it were, to make their position more odious, arguments were daily promulgated, and very generally, from the press throughout the State, based upon the further groundless assumption, that the issue, then pending, was separate secession or submission. The *Standard* did not choose to be bound by pledges which, as it alleged, the State never made, nor to accept an issue which it regarded as unfair and deceptive, and, therefore, the publication of the paper was put forth in defence of the principles of themselves and their party, which were that the State was bound by the action of her General Assembly up to 1850, to await the action of the other Southern States.

The *Standard* was successful, in the fall of 1851, in bringing about a test vote by the people, as to whether South Carolina should alone sever her connection with the Union, or whether the Southern States should act conjointly. The result of this vote was against separate secession, and the State Convention, which had been previously elected, adopted a compromise course.

In October, 1852, five more prominent gentlemen became associated with the founders of the *Standard*, and a stock company was formed—the first instance with the Charleston press, subsequent to 1828. The stock company of the *Standard* was composed of Messrs. KER BOYCE, M. C.

MORDECAI, B. C. PRESSLEY, L. W. SPRATT, E. H. BRIT-
TON, W. D. PORTER, JAMES TUPPER, and JACOB COHEN.
The combined wealth of the individual shareholders, was
estimated at six millions of dollars.

Mr. B. C. PRESSLEY, withdrew from the editorial chair,
June 14, 1853. His mantle fell, gracefully, on L. W.
SPRATT. For about eight months the paper was published
by SPRATT, BRITTON & Co. Those facile editors—B. C.
PRESSLEY, L. W. SPRATT, J. L. HATCH, and the very
practical and energetic E. H. BRITTON, gave to that paper—
the title of which was changed in October, 1853, to *The
Charleston Standard*—their untiring devotion, and as newspaper editors, did much in limiting the range of errors.

Mr. BRITTON began his apprenticeship to the business
in the office of *The City Gazette*, and finished his time in
the office of the *Mercury*. He left Charleston and went to
Columbia, in this State, in 1840, and there, in 1847, revived *The Southern Chronicle*. He removed to Winns-
boro' in 1848, and published *The Fairfield Herald and
Register*. He returned to Charleston in 1853, as associate
proprietor and editor of the *Standard*. He returned to
Columbia and bought out *The Columbia Times*. Mr.
BRITTON has since settled finally in Charlotte, North Carolina, where he established *The Charlotte Bulletin*, which
he is still conducting.

Mr. S. R. CROCKER, who edited the paper after Mr.
HATCH, in consort with J. D. BUDDS, its business manager
and collector, struggled persistently, though unsuccessful-
ly, to sustain it. The *Standard* was not published after
June 25, 1858. Messrs. PRESSLEY and SPRATT had before
that period, confined themselves, exclusively, to the practice of the law, which has since given them their deserved
celebrity. Mr. CROCKER returned to his home in New
England. He is now the publisher of *The Literary World*,

a monthly journal of Boston, Massachusetts. Mr. BUDDS became devoted to the interests of the *Mercury*, down to the period of the forced discontinuance of that journal.

WILLIAM D. CLANCY, was, for a brief period, near the close of 1857, assistant editor of the *Standard*. His connection with that paper, was not sufficiently long, however, to experience the reality that although cares, responsibilities and fatigues had to be encountered, the position of editor had, nevertheless, its rose-hued pleasures.

Mr. HATCH, of whom mention has already been made, was from New-Gloucester, in the State of Maine He was a young man of much energy and talent ; one of the swiftest of stenographers, and reported in full, for the *Standard*, the memorable Æriel murder case, which took place in February, 1856. He also reported and published, in pamphlet form, " Rights of Corporators and Reporters," being a lengthy report of the case of " R. W. GIBBES, editor of the Columbia *South Carolinian*, vs. E. J. ARTHUR, Mayor of Columbia, S. C., and JOHN BURDELL, Chief of Police," which was tried in the Court of Common Pleas, for Richland District, March term, 1857. It was an issue made by Dr. GIBBES, with the City Council of Columbia, as to the right of a citizen to attend their public meetings, and report their proceedings, if he saw fit.

A poignant attack in the *Standard* of 23d July, 1856—the work of Mr. HATCH's pen, editor *pro tem*, in the absence of Mr. SPRATT—severely animadverted upon the political expressions of Colonel JOHN CUNNINGHAM, then editor of *The Evening News*. Mr. HATCH, though by birth a New Englander, had become strongly Southern in his political sentiment, and conceived that the editor of *The Evening News* had spoken uncivilly of the course taken by the Southern delegation then in Washington, "insinuating," Mr. HATCH said, " that our delegation in

Congress have done nothing, and can do nothing that will contribute to or consist with the welfare of the State, that—in its mildest form of expression—they have exhibited a want of statesmanship. Moreover, that the members of this same delegation have been influenced in their public conduct by a consideration of the spoils." This was during the BROOKS and SUMNER embroglio. The caustic leader in the *Standard*, met with a taunting response from the *News*. This led to a correspondence between the two editors, which terminated in a hostile meeting. The encounter, which took place in close proximity to the Washington Race Course, was bloodless, and after an exchange of shots, an amicable adjustment of the difficulty was effected.

Mr. HATCH fell a victim to the epidemic of 1858—the yellow fever—dying on the 25th September, of that year, in the 26th year of his age. The skillful medical treatment and personal attention of Doctor PETER PORCHER, at whose home Mr. HATCH was staying, could not prevent the death of one, who, had he lived, could not but have been prominent as a journalist. That gallant corps, the Washington Light Infantry, of which he was a member, took charge of the body of their comrade, and deposited it in their sepulchre at "Magnolia." They were, subsequently, removed to a neighboring spot, in the same "city of the dead."

CHAPTER XVII.

WE have purposely avoided speaking of the few Quarterly, and of the several Monthly and Weekly publications—six of the latter will be excepted—which from time
to time were issued, and to which the struggle of 1812, was
instrumental in giving life and vigor. They were too
ephemeral, to have a place in this history. If we omit
three, it is likewise the case with the Periodical Press of
Charleston, which, in its purport, is not the less effective.
Of this more elementary branch, we no not propose to
speak.

The six hebdomadals, however, were solid, and outlived
opposition. They were *The United States Catholic Miscellany, The Wesleyan Journal, The Southern Christian
Sentinel, The Charleston Observer, The Southern Presbyterian, and The Southern Baptist.*

The *Miscellany* came into existence under the control and editorship of the Right Reverend Doctor JOHN ENG- LAND, first Bishop of the Roman Catholic Diocese of Charleston, on the 5th June, 1822. For some cause not now known, the *Miscellany* was discontinued, but was re- sumed after an interval of one year, on the 7th January, 1824.

A writer in the *Courier*, who signed himself "A Metho- dist," thus alluded to Bishop ENGLAND'S discourse, in fa- vor of the Greek's, delivered Sunday, 25th January, 1824 : "The picture which Bishop ENGLAND drew of Grecian misery, was calculated to move the coldest enemy of liber- ty and religion."

The *Miscellany*, which was printed at different times by THOMAS MARTIN, jr., JOHN HEALEY, JEREMIAH DENNE- HY, WILLIAM J. MOSEMANN, WALKER & JAMES, and last- ly by the then well known firm of HARPER & CALVO, had among the priesthood, many able contributors. The most prominent were Bishops ENGLAND and REYNOLDS, Reve- rend R. S. BAKER, Vicar General under Bishop ENGLAND, Reverend J. F. O'NEILL, Very Reverend Doctors CORCO- RAN and LYNCH—the latter now the highly intellectual and esteemed Bishop of the Diocese, appointed to the See of Charleston, in January, 1858—and BIRMINGHAM, the present Vicar General, and others.

Bishop ENGLAND'S chief literary labors were bestowed upon the paper he was so devoted to. Its editorial columns were continually supplied with the fruits of his clear and gifted intellect.

JOHN ENGLAND was born in the City of Cork, 23d Sep- tember, 1786. At an early period he entered the College of Maynooth, in the vicinity of the Irish metropolis ; after leaving college he placed himself under the tutorship of an eminent barrister, with whom he studied law for about two years. He then relinquished the legal profession for the ministry, and entered the Theological College of Carlow, where he completed his ecclesiastical course of studies with distinction. He was ordained a priest in 1808, at the early age of 22, and entered on the duties of the ministry in Cork.

This young priest, with eight different functions already enjoined upon him, became the editor of the Cork *Morning Chronicle*, in which office he mastered the typographical art. "With the same promptness to perceive, and daring to perform, which always marked his subsequent course, he wielded his pen in one bold denunciation of the moral degradation of his unhappy country, the corruption of judges, and the packing of juries. He stemmed the political torrent which had already swept before it, many that were dear to him. In that denunciation, this patriot priest made issue with the tory Lord Lieutenant Earl TALBOT, the English representative. Though this Catholic editor had, in that article, engraven upon the people their rights, it was, nevertheless, at a cost of five hundred pounds." The Court before which, he was summoned, in addition to the fine, decreed, also, his close confinement, until the pecuniary penalty was paid. So firmly did the people determine to protect these rights, that the mother of Mr. ENGLAND, from the gallery of ladies above, at the close of her son's masterly defence, exclaimed : " Well done, my dear son. In my hand I have a check for the amount ; write but another essay, expose again the tyranny of the persecutors of your church, and your country, and I shall meet the forfeit, though it be double the amount of this !"

This editor and priest is said to have allowed his name to be placed among those who were willing to go forth to new fields of labor. But he affixed this condition, that he should be sent to some country over which the English held no control. This proviso to the priest's name, attracted the attention of Pope Pius 7th, at the time a new See for the Carolina's and Georgia was about being made. The Pope knew the priest's record, and appointed him, in 1820, to the new prelacy, though only in his thirty-fourth year. He came from Belfast, in the ship *Thomas Getston*, and arrived in Charleston, on the last day of that year. Under these circumstances was it, that this man, whose name is one of the proudest in the list of prelates, distinguished for strength of mind, power of argument, deep and various learning, and a bold and impressive eloquence, was transferred to our, *then*, unoppressed land, and became one of the literary ornaments of our City.

In private life also, this distinguished editor was greatly esteemed, and the author well remembers how wonderful was the charm he threw around it. He possessed a nature, warm and overflowing to a class who revered him. And yet, the regard for him was not bounded by monastic vows or rules, for among the immense throng who visited the remains, until the interment of this pious defender of his church, there were to be seen the Catholic, the Hebrew, the Episcopalian, the Lutheran, the Baptist, the Congregationalist, the Methodist, the Universalist, the Unitarian, and the Presbyterian—the various sects into which our people are divided. Bishop ENGLAND was taken from his field of labors, by the Providence of God, on the 11th April, 1842, in the 56th year of his age.

The *Miscellany* was printed in octavo form, and was the first regular organ of the Catholics in the United States, receiving as it did, the support of Catholics, generally, throughout America. It was changed to a super-royal sheet in 1824. It was, at that time, the strong advocate for a modification of the laws then in force against aliens, before they could possibly acquire the benefits of citizenship. Its discontinuance was owing entirely to the destruction of all its material, in the great fire of December, 1861.

The first Methodist weekly newspaper published in the South, and the second, in point of time, in the United States, was published in Charleston, under the title of *The Wesleyan Journal.* It was projected by the late distinguished STEPHEN OLIN, D.D., then a resident of this State, and subsequently, President of the Wesleyan University. The South Carolina Conference then embraced Georgia, and this body adopted the *Journal* as its organ, and made arrangements for a more extended publication. *The Wesleyan Journal* made its debut on the 1st October, 1825, under the editorial supervision of Reverend Doctor WILLIAM CAPERS, of South Carolina. The health of Doctor OLIN having failed him, it was, after a couple of years, merged in *The Christian Advocate,* a coherent journal which was started in New York, during the autumn of 1826; thence it was, that it took the title of *Christian Advocate and Journal.* The lapse of ten years showed that a great central organ at New York, however ably conducted, could not supersede the home demand for religious literature and representation. Accordingly, resolutions were adopted at the General Conference, held at Cincinnati, Ohio, in 1836, authorizing the publication, in this City, of a weekly religious journal, called *Southern Christian Advocate.* Doctor WILLIAM CAPERS was elected as editor. The first number was published June 21, 1837. The paper had no printing office, but was " worked off" at the job printing establishment of Mr. JAMES S. BURGES; and the editor acted as his own clerk. The *Advocate* came out, in form, vastly superior to *The Wesleyan Journal.* The leading editorials were more elaborate, the selections more varied, and adapted to the popular taste. Doctor CAPERS stood up, firmly,

15

for the rights of his portion of the ecclesiastical connection. "He was earnest," says his biographer, "and high-minded in his advocacy of all the great measures subscribing to the spread of Christian influence—educational, missionary, and literary. But he did not *warm* to a work which was not, to him, a labor of love."

At the General Conference, held in Baltimore, in May, 1840, Doctor CAPERS resigned the editorship of the paper. He was succeeded by Reverend Doctor WM. M. WIGHTMAN, who was, by the same Conference, appointed his successor. Dr. WIGHTMAN entered upon his duties in November, 1840. During the interval, Reverend Doctor WHITEFOORD SMITH, who was then stationed in the City, assumed the editorial chair *pro tem.* Dr. WIGHTMAN was a native of Charleston, and a graduate of the College of Charleston. He had youth and enterprise in his favor; wielded a facile and polished pen. With the increasing income of the paper, an office was fitted up in Pinckney Street, and a HOE's cylinder press purchased, and the regular routine of a first class journal was entered upon. Subsequently—June 7, 1850—the press was propelled by steam. It was the second application of this motive power to newspaper press-work in this City.

In 1844, the Methodist Episcopal Church was divided, by mutual consent, into its present Northern and Southern organizations. During the perilous times which ensued, the *Southern Christian Advocate* was one of the great sheet-anchors of the South. The judicious course of the editor was commended by the General Conference.

BENJAMIN JENKINS, a native of Bermuda, was the first foreman of the *Advocate*. He quitted a similar position in the office of *The Charleston Courier*, to accept that, a less arduous one. He was a good Hebraist and classical scholar; was master of the principal modern languages, and, alike, master of his own business. Having been appointed a missionary to China, he took orders in 1848, and sailed from Boston to Shanghai. He subsequently held the position of Interpreter in the United States Consulate General. Mr. C. CANNING, of Ireland, succeeded Doctor JENKINS, in the foremanship of the *Advocate*, and still retains the position.

In 1850, Reverend Doctor THOMAS O. SUMMERS, an Englishman by birth, was appointed assistant editor of the *Advocate*, and was associated with it four years. His critical acumen, and sensitive poetic taste, with his varied attainments, were acquisitions to the journal. The sheet was enlarged, and the subscription list extended, at the time Doctor WIGHTMAN's term of service—fourteen years—closed. While recognized as the fearless defender of evangelical religion, according to the views of the denomination of Christians whom it represented, its tone was always courteous, its spirit genial, and the ability of its editorials sustained; in fact, it became a power in religious journalism.

When Doctor WIGHTMAN accepted the Presidency of Wofford College, in 1854, the Reverend Doctor E. H. MYERS, of Georgia, was elected his successor, in the editorial management of the paper. This Divine brought energy and business talent to sustain its financial department. The paper was again enlarged, and removed to apartments more commodious, in Hayne Street. During the desolation consequent upon the late war, it was deemed advisable to remove the office of publication to Augusta, Georgia. Subsequently, it was removed to Macon, Georgia. The war having left it without any resources that would insure its continuance, it was sold to Messrs. J. W. BURKE & Co., prominent publishers of that City, and by whom it is at present published. The *Advocate* is a double sheet, of

eight columns each, measuring 29 by 22 inches, and printed
in the best style, on excellent paper.

The Charleston Observer was the organ of the Presbyte-
rians, and was established by the Reverend BENJAMIN
GILDERSLEEVE, who came to Charleston from Hancock
County, Georgia. It was conducted by the members of the
Charleston Union Presbytery. The leading object of this
publication, was to make its readers early acquainted with
the progress of the Redeemer's kingdom, at home and
abroad ; both as it related to the labors, and conflicts of his
servants, on the one hand, and the gracious influences of
his spirit, on the other. Assurances were at the same
time given to its patrons, by the editor, that while carrying
out this benign design, he would also communicate such
information representing the affairs of government, and the
advancement of literature and science, as an enlightened
mind would desire to receive. Prominent as writers in
support of this weekly, were B. M. PALMER, D.D., A. W.
LELAND, D.D., F. C. HENRY, D.D., Reverend W. A. Mc-
DOWALL, and Reverend A. BUIST.

The first appearance of the *Observer* was in July, 1826.
It was issued regularly in Charleston, from the office of the
paper, Chalmers Street, near Meeting Street, until the 26th
July, 1845. On the 8th August, of the same year, its proprietor, who stood high among the Titans of controversy,
changed its place of publication to Richmond, Virginia,
there to be united with *The Watchman of the South*. It
was issued from that City as *The Watchman and Observer*,
August 21, 1845. The change impaired its vitality, and
in Richmond it died, but a few years before the war. Mr.
GILDERSLEEVE now lives, in his declining years, in the
"Old Dominion." Mr. JOHN CUDWORTH, a practical printer of this City, and one who has, long ago, laid aside the
implements of the craft, was his foreman and general su-

perintendent, for full nineteen years—the length of time it was published in Charleston. In the office of that paper, the present foreman of the *Courier*, Mr. ORAN BASSETT, well known to the craft, served his apprenticeship.

The Southern Christian Sentinel made its appearance in Charleston, March 2d, 1839. Reverend THOMAS MAGRUDER, a Georgian by birth, was editor, assisted by Reverend W. C. DANA. The *Sentinel* was the organ of the Charleston Union Presbytery, during the agitation consequent on the disruption of the Presbyterian Church, in the United States, by certain acts of the Assembly in 1837–'38. The Charleston Union Presbytery had disapproved those acts, as being "unconstitutional and unjust." This disapproval was imputed to them as a crime; and they were denied their rights as members of the Synod. But Providence destined for them a signal and almost unexampled vindication of the rectitude of their course. The "Old School" General Assembly of 1852, meeting in Charleston, and becoming acquainted with the facts, re-instated them in their rights; and lately, the whole Presbyterian community— "Old School" and "New"—at the North, where the "unpleasantness" originated, have given the strongest proof of their disapproval of those acts, by becoming again one Church.

Reverend THOMAS MAGRUDER was a man of the purest integrity and honor, incapable of indirection, and uniting with a guileless nature, inflexible adherence to principle. It was impossible for him to be an unscrupulous partisan, or a narrow-minded bigot. In Christian simplicity and transparency of character, he resembled another firm friend and ally of the *Sentinel*—the late Reverend Dr. B. M. PALMER, once pastor of the Circular Church.

The closing years of Mr. MAGRUDER's life were spent in Madison County, Mississippi, where property had been left him by a near relative. As long as declining years permitted, he preached, for the most part gratuitously, and with great acceptance. He died in 1853. A beautiful tribute was paid to his memory, by those who, taking "sweet counsel" with him as a clerical brother, had learned to appreciate his solid mental qualities, and his great moral worth.

Reverend W. C. DANA, whose pen freely contributed in aid of the *Sentinel,* was born in Newburyport, Massachusetts, in 1810; graduated at Dartmouth College, New Hampshire. He completed his theological studies in Andover; spent one session at Princeton, and, several at Columbia, in this State. He was, in November, 1835, called to the Third Presbyterian—now Central—Church of this City, and is the devout and much loved pastor of that Congregation.

The *Southern Christian Sentinel* was originated as a local and temporary necessity; it was not expected to be self-sustaining. Generously aided by a few friends, and edited gratuitously, it was continued as a weekly paper through the years 1839–'40; and as a monthly periodical, to the end of 1841. In its valedictory were quoted these prophetic lines:

> "Truth, crushed to earth, shall live again;
> The eternal years of God are her's;
> But error, wounded, writhes in pain,
> And dies, amid her worshipers."

The *Southern Presbyterian,* the most variable of the hebdomadals, was first published at Milledgeville, Georgia, and edited by Reverend WASHINGTON BAIRD, before it was removed to Charleston. After twelve months publication, it was sold to a company composed of JOSEPH A. ENSLOW, JOHN M. FRASER, WILLIAM HARRAL, JAMES M. CALDWELL, and others. It was then printed and issued by that well known printer, JOHN B. NIXON, in Meeting Street, next South of the Hibernian Hall. Subsequently, early in 1856, ARCHIBALD CAMPBELL became the manager, and directed it for the said share holders, until the spring of 1857, when he relinquished the position, to assume the duties of City Treasurer.

ARCHIBALD CAMPBELL was born in Greenock, Scotland, August, 1799. He was the only son of ROBERT CAMPBELL, of the British Navy. ARCHIBALD CAMPBELL will be remembered as an able, pure and just man. These attributes enabled him to hold, for nearly thirty years of his life, the offices of clerk of the Court, and Commissioner of Equity for Beaufort District. He died at Summerville, October 21, 1866. The editors, at that period, were Reverend J. L. KIRKPATRICK and Reverend B. LANNEAU. About 1857, Reverend Dr. W. M. CUNNINGHAM assumed the editorship, and published it at the printing office of Messrs. JAMES & WILLIAMS, at No. 16 State Street, nearly opposite Chalmers Street. Early in the war, the material was removed to Columbia, and while there, Reverend A. A. PORTER took editorial charge of the paper. Finally, it passed under the control of Reverend JOHN B. ADGER and ELAM SHARP. The title of this religious weekly has been changed to *Southern Presbyterian Index*, and is now in successful operation at the State Capital, under the superintendence and editorship of Reverend JAMES WOODROW, D.D.

The last, though by no means the least of these weekly prints, was *The Southern Baptist*. This paper was started in the fall of 1839, by Reverend T. W. HAINES, a native of Tennessee. He was its publisher and editor, assisted for about two years by Reverend WILLIAM T. BRANTLY, D.D., and Reverend THOMAS CURTIS, D.D.

Doctor BRANTLY was one of the earliest students of the South Carolina College, having graduated with distinction, in 1808. He was a man of enlarged and cultivated mind; delighting equally in the walks of literature and science. A holy man of God, eminently useful in his vocation and generation; more beloved, the more intimately known. He was stricken with paralysis, which affected both mind and body. He died in Augusta—whither he had removed, in the hope of alleviating his suffering condition—February 28, 1849.

Doctor CURTIS, was an Englishman, of the old school, perfected by the crowning graces and influences of humble, fervent and exemplary piety. For many years before he came to America, he was a leading reporter of the debates in the English Parliament. He came to this country about the year 1833, and settled in Bangor, Maine. In 1841, he accepted a pastoral call for the Wentworth Street (Second) Baptist Church, of this City. This Divine attained eminent distinction in the world of letters, and found ready access into high literary circles. While in Charleston, he took great interest, and actively co-operated in the formation of a Society for the observance of the Lord's day. He likewise, took an active part in the formation of the Southern Baptist Convention, held in the City of Augusta, in May, 1845, and ever manifested a lively interest in all institutions of charity and benevolence. Doctor CURTIS lost his life on board of the *North Carolina*, one of the Bay Line steamers, while she was making her trip from Baltimore to Norfolk, on the night of January 28, 1859.

The *Baptist*, in the spring of 1849, passed into the hands of a Committee, who became managers and editors. Reverend J. R. KENDRICK, B. C. PRESSLEY and JAMES TUPPER, composed the Committee. From 1848 to the spring of 1849, Reverend JAS. P. BOYCE edited it for the Committee, with great vigor, and contributed his private means in its aid. During the successful career of this journal,

Reverend E. T. WINKLER, D.D., ably presided over its editorial department. In a controversy conducted by him at that time, his pen gave evidence of great erudition. The *Baptist* was, at a later period, edited by other pleasing and talented writers, the Reverend J. P. TUSTIN and the Reverend W. B. CARSON. Its suspension occurred while it was under the management of Reverend Mr. CARSON, not from any want of capacity, but from unavoidable circumstances.

CHAPTER XVIII.

THE author has brought down and blended history and
biography quite up to the opening of the year 1871. The
want of a more extended record prevents him from entering upon similar details in regard to the present representatives of local journalism.

They constitute the following: *The Charleston Daily
News*, which paper was presented to its patrons and the
public through the instrumentality of BENJAMIN WOOD,
GEORGE R. CATHCART, JAMES W. MCMILLAN and MAN-
DRED MORTON, on the morning of August 14, 1865. Mr.
WOOD was the proprietor of *The Daily News*, of New
York; Mr. CATHCART, a native of Spartanburg County, in
this State, and was, at the time, the New York correspond-
ent of the London *Morning Post;* Mr. MCMILLAN, a
Charlestonian, and a very practical member of the craft,
and Mr. MORTON, said to be a nephew of Mr. WOOD. Mr.
WOOD supplied the means for the enterprise. To Mr.
CATHCART was assigned the responsible duties of editor,
and to Mr. MCMILLAN was apportioned the exacting duties
of business manager. Mr. MORTON, unlike his co-partners,
was entirely unknown to the fraternity of editors in the

City. Quite dissimilar to any other Charleston daily, previously published, no line of policy was marked out for this paper. It was, of course, to be a Southern journal, representing Southern interests, but it was not to be under the control of any one man or party, other than was deemed advisable by the editor. The *News* was established at a period favorable to the undertaking, and under the editorship of GEORGE R. CATHCART, assisted by L. W. SPRATT, A. G. MAGRATH, W. H. TRESCOTT, J. BARRETT COHEN, JAMES LOWNDES, Dr. H. BAER, ROSWELL T. LOGAN, and JOHN D. MILLER, the paper acquired prosperity and popularity as it went forth from the office of publication, 18 Hayne Street. In October, 1867, the co-partnership of CATHCART, McMILLAN & MORTON was dissolved, and the entire management of the paper devolved upon Messrs. RIORDAN, DAWSON & CO.

B. R. RIORDAN is the senior of the firm now conducting *The Charleston Daily News.* He was born in Fairfax County, State of Virginia, in 1839. He graduated at Mt. St. Mary's College, Maryland, in 1858. It was in the office of the Washington *Union* that he received his newspaper training. In 1859, he became connected with the editorial staff of the New Orleans *Delta.* He was sent by the proprietors of that journal to represent their paper in the Democratic National Convention, which assembled in this City, April 23, 1860, and came with the delegation, in the steam ship *Coatzacoalcas.* In the summer of 1860, he became connected with *The Charleston Mercury,* and on the retirement of GEORGE A. GORDON, in September of the same year, he accepted the position of managing editor of that paper; there he remained until just before the evacuation of Charleston. Since the war, he was, for nearly a year, on the staff of the Richmond *Examiner.* In the winter of 1866, he accepted position as one of the assistant editors of the *Courier*, and continued in that capacity until shortly before he became one of the proprietors of the *News*.

F. W. Dawson, of the *News*, was born in London, Eng land, in 1840. At the time of the breaking out of the war between the Confederate States and the Federal Union, he was engaged on the editorial staff of a London newspaper. In December, 1861, he enlisted at Southampton, England, as a sailor on the Confederate steam ship *Nashville*. On the arrival of the steamer at Beaufort, North Carolina, early in 1862, he was appointed a Master's Mate in the Navy of the new Confederacy. This position he resigned in June, 1862, and joined the "Purcell Battery," Hill's Division, Army of Northern Virginia, as a private. In August, 1862, he was commissioned First Lieutenant of Artillery, and assigned to duty as ordnance officer, on the staff of General Longstreet. In the spring of 1864, he was promoted to a Captaincy of Artillery, and in the fall of the same year, was tranferred to the staff of General Fitz Hugh Lee, where he served until the end of the war. When the Richmond *Examiner* was revived in 1865, Mr. Dawson became one of its "Local Reporters." After the *Examiner* had been suppressed by the United States military authorities, Mr. Dawson accepted a position among the corps of editors of the Richmond *Dispatch*, and held it until the fall of 1866, when he became the assistant editor of *The Charleston Mercury*, as previously mentioned, November 19, 1866. This position he held until October, 1867, when he became one of the proprietors and editors of *The Charleston Daily News*.

The first "City Editor" of the *Daily News*, was the popular paragraphist and humorist, James H. Simmons. His ready pen, which has given much aid to this journal, was first recognized in the columns of *The South Carolinian*,

16

when it was resumed in Charleston, in January, 1866. The *Carolinian* having suspended in the summer of that year, Mr. SIMMONS accepted the "Local" chair of the *News*, then conducted by Messrs. CATHCART, McMILLAN & MORTON. He was indefatigable in the discharge of his duties, and known for the "lightness of his brow," and the dawning smile of pleasantry in his countenance, uniting humor with seriousness, and, seemingly, caring for nothing so much as a mirth-moving jest. He was succeeded in this department of the office by F. D. LEE, who was called from the office of the Savannah *News*, in June, 1869. Mr. LEE—after his association with the paper which lasted until October, 1870—quitted the "Local" chair for another field of usefulness, in the City of Augusta, Georgia.

The South Carolina Leader was the production of TIMOTHY HURLEY. T. HURLEY & Co. were, after the first few numbers, announced as the publishers, and ALLEN COFFIN was recognized as the editor. The first number of this weekly appeared Saturday, October 7, 1865, from their office, 430 King Street. In the salutatory article of the paper its patrons were informed that it would be devoted to the interests of "Free Labor and General Reform." Its motto was from ST. MARK, 4th chapter, 28th verse: "First the blade, then the ear, after that, the full corn in the ear." Before the (y)ear filled, the dream of Mr. HURLEY had flitted away. The *Leader* became mutable in its proprietorship, until the spring of 1867, when it became the property of a stock company, at the head of which was the Reverend R. H. CAIN, with A. J. RANSIER as the editor. Its title was changed April 7, 1868, to *The Missionary Record*. R. H. CAIN, who is now the publisher and editor, is a colored preacher of the Gospel; he has, measurably, modified the ultra proclivities of the paper. R. H. CAIN is a native of Greenbrier County, Virginia, and came

to Charleston from New York City, in April, 1865. The
Record is still published and edited by him, at the office
in Morris Street.

The South Carolina Republican was also a weekly newspaper. It was founded October 10, 1868, and after two
other weeklies, *The Free Press*, and *The Charleston Advocate* had each run a very brief career. The suspension of
these two latter papers, left no "blank in nature."

The founders of the *Republican* were J. M. MORRIS and
MYRON FOX. Mr. MORRIS graduated at "Yale" with the
highest valedictory honors, and before he reached the age
of 33, was prominent in political organizations, between
the years 1865 and '68. He became the boldest champion
of Republican principles in South Carolina. Mr. FOX has
given evidences of fine intellectual endowment, and his
scholar-like editorials in defence of the principles of his
paper, were calculated to sustain the dignity and worth of
the Charleston press.

The first place of publication of the *Republican* was at
the printing office of Messrs. DENNY & PERRY. Subsequently, it was removed to the North-East corner of Meeting and Calhoun Streets; thence to its present site, where,
on the 19th August, 1869, their daily first appeared. Both
the weekly and the daily—the latter now enjoying a mo-
nopoly of afternoon intelligence—were established in the
interest of the Republican Party, by the individuals named, and during the periods above mentioned. It is now
issued from the building South-West corner of Market and
Meeting Streets. The assistant editors are R. H. WIL-
LOUGHBY and E. G. HOFFMAN. In Mr. CHARLES SAMMIS,
the business manager, there are combined candor, and
sound common sense, qualities conducive to the success of
a daily newspaper.

The organ of the German population, is *The Suedlicher*

Correspondent. It was established by C. G. ERCKMAN, in
January, 1869. Its place of publication is on North side
of Broad Street, two doors West of Church Street. It is
the third of the German organs, strictly national in representation, known in the City. The first, *The Teutone,* was
started by JOHN A. WAGNER, in 1844. It was then printed South side of Broad Street, West of the Guard House.
The Teutone became by purchase, the property of F. MEL-
CHERS, in October, 1853. The latter proprietor changed
its title to *The Zeitung,* at that time. From that period
until the State called her sons to arms in 1861, Mr. MEL-
CHERS conducted this Teutonic semi-weekly, not only ably,
but quite successfully. In January, 1871, *The Zeitung*
was revived by F. MELCHERS & SON. General JOHN A.
WAGNER, and Captain F. MELCHERS have largely contributed to the editorial columns of *The Teutone, The
Suedlicher Correspondent,* and *The Deutsche Zeitung,* three
newspapers which have deservedly received the approba-
tion and support of our thriving German population.

The Referee, weekly—E. DURBEC, proprietor, was established June 12, 1869. It is printed at the office of the
paper, 235 King Street, and distributed gratis, the publisher depending solely upon the advertising patronage of
a paper, which is in size, only 23 by 32.

The Southern Celt, an Irish-American hebdomadal, was
established in January, 1870; L. C. NORTHROP was the
first editor and proprietor. *The Celt* was formerly *The
Gazette,* a Catholic organ, which was established by Messrs.
CAULFIELD & FORD, in January, 1866. That firm sold to
Bishop LYNCH, who purchased it for J. D. BUDDS ; Father
J. D. QUIGLEY was the editor, and the printer was that
experienced member of the craft, CONN O'NEALE. The
Celt is now published by JAMES BRENNAN, and is issued

weekly from the printing establishment of *The Daily Republican.*

The Sunday Times is another weekly, as its title denotes. This paper, which is published in Hayne Street by J. W. DELANO, made its bow for public patronage on the morning of Sunday, 20th March, 1870.

The last newspaper, and one which has just taken its place on the list of hebdomadal publications of Charleston, is that called *The Working Christian.* It was established in the interest of the Baptist denomination, at Yorkville, South Carolina, by Reverend TILMAN R. GAINES. In May, 1870, it was removed to this City. *The Working Christian* is issued from 68 Hasel Street.

To allude further to our contemporary press, would be invidious and uncalled for. The living journals of the day speak for themselves, through the work and bearing of those who control them. But beginning, as it were, a new epoch, emerging from ruins under the most embarrassing influences of political and pecuniary affairs, it will be well to refer the craft, to the examples we have given of their predecessors.

CHAPTER XIX.

THE amount of material of an historical nature that accumulates gradually on the files of a daily journal, is astounding, and would scarcely be realized by any but persons whose habitudes and necessities of research have led them frequently to explore such sources. Appreciating this fact to more than an ordinary extent, we are struck with the reality that the press which chronicles all things, often over-looks its *own* exploits and triumphs.

While upon this topic, we would suggest that our Carolina press might in more respects become auto-biographical, and relate its own experience. In other words, might not important and interesting additions be made to our State history, if each County journal now extant, would furnish a full and authentic narrative of its establishment and location of the press in its section? Landmarks might thus be established, so that hence the retrospective observer of the progress of the State, as well as its journalistic efforts would not meet with difficulties akin to those that have beset one who has endeavored to ascertain how matters stood one hundred and forty years ago.

There was one feature, beautiful indeed, in the life of journalism in our halcyon days, which should be revived. It was the fraternal spirit in which our predecessors lived and met together; their frequent re-unions; their chivalrous deportment; the amenity and courteousness with which they wrote, precluded provocation, to the most sensitive nature. They sustained, as has been said, a perfect organization among themselves, which, socially, was rarely ruptured. They took no undue advantage of each other, reciprocated all courtesies, and were, especially, above the fault of competing with each other's prices, for the sake of temporary gain, to the common loss of all, and to the disparagement of the profession. Courtesy is one of the exacting conditions in the life of a profession like that of journalism, which may be said to "live, move, and have its being," in armor.

The tone and temper of the Charleston press, in that era of good feeling, has been very correctly depicted by a writer who has signed himself "S. G." That writer we take to be the late talented and courteous Divine, SAMUEL GILMAN, D.D., in whose language dissimulation found no resting place. "S. G." thus marked the course of the press in a letter written from Charleston, in the summer of 1842:

"In my early impressions" wrote "S. G.," "nothing struck me more pleasantly, than the air of high-bred courtesy which characterized the intercourse of the public journals with each other; and though I have been a daily reader of the *Courier*, *Mercury* and *Patriot*, I have never read in their papers a gross allusion, or an indelicate remark; nor, though I perceive they are diametrically antagonistic in political sentiment, has one indulged towards the other in bitter invective, or violent animosity. I can attribute this to no cause but the refinement which is, certainly, peculiar to Charleston."

Frequent intercourse, and interchange of sentiment are, doubtless, advantageous to the mutual interests of 'the press. There can be no reason why the example set by our predecessors should not be observed by the proprietors and editors of newspapers, not only those of the City, but by the press of the State, at large; for it has a high mission to perform, and responsible duties to discharge.

Editors occasionally show themselves careless of that courtesy which is due to contributors, who deserve, and should receive respect, even if their desires are not strictly complied with; to the public, to whom the deportment of an editor should ever be the model of propriety, politeness, and the most graceful social observances. Time and again have we seen in days past, individuals who demanded to be heard through the columns of one of the papers, depart from the sanctum of the editor, fully convinced that the responsive monosyllable no! so affably given, covered a comprehensive reasoning, which they did not at first perceive. This is a style of courtesy which should be first in the vocabulary of journalism, and is known only to the true editor. This lesson is important, when it is considered that in working out the duties of journalism, the business is of such a nature as perpetually to demand the exercise of a gentlemanly and Christian amenity.

It is admitted that there is no vocation which may more easily be perverted to the indulgence of spite, malice, dislike, and a rivally which too frequently ends in prejudices never to be subdued. These evils are due to many causes, the greatest of them being a diseased eagerness for gain. When the competition is great, and the profit meagre, this, as is well known, is one of the fruitful causes which bring into life the evil demon of egotism and self-seeking. The danger is that this demon will acquire strength daily, especially, it is to be feared, among the diurnal press, South of that geographical and political boundary line which was first made memorable to all America, by CHARLES MASON and JEREMIAH DIXON, one hundred and seven years ago. And yet, if the true and faithful editors of the South would pause and reflect, they would discover that it is just now of

more importance to them than all else beside, that they
should work, with one common will, to instruct mankind;
to spread correct information; to promote the cause of
virtue; to support the dignity of law—now, more than
ever, needed; to meliorate the heart, thereby elevating the
mind. Let them link hands, and say one to another, I
know but the South—the South emerging from her ruins!

It is manifestly proper, that we should here draw the
attention of the craft to an endowment not a great while
ago perfected, having for its object the training of young
men to the business—we should properly say, craft of journalism.

While acknowledging the generous and liberal temper
which prompted such an endowment, the author must be
allowed to remark that a long acquaintance with journalism in general leads him to question, very seriously, the
uses of any specialty of training. Indeed we find it diffi-
cult to conceive, through what peculiar course of tuition
one could proceed to arrive at the knowledge of a profession, which, almost beyond all others, demands, not only a
specialty of gift in the individual, and singularly various
knowledge, but likewise, a long experience with the nature,
the wants and the wishes of society. There are, also, great
and conflicting principles and doctrines, involving a con-
flict, not only of years, but of ages. It does seem to us,
all that can be done, to prepare a youth at college, for the
business of journalism, is what the college now proposes to
do, in the work of a classical education. In this, the youth
is prepared generally for all the professions, and no college
training can possibly do more. It certainly cannot go into
the thousand details which enter into the business of the
journalist. It surely cannot *endow* the individual with
those gifts of intellect which are special, and should belong
to the journalist. Nor can such an education accomplish

more than perfect him in the languages, in the sciences, and in general literature. The school for the journalist—assuming that he has acquired all that the college usually imparts, and that he possesses the necessary gifts from nature—is the great world-school of humanity. Professors might lecture on journalism, as it is practically known to the craft, day succeeding day, and yet these censors of wisdom would not impart any journalistic lesson to the student. The embryo journalist would still have to go through a regular apprenticeship to the craft, and acquire the essential knowledge by hard practice. These lessons, experience has taught us, are to be found in the thoroughfares—in the strife of parties—at public meetings, and under the glare of midnight gas.

The editorial management of the various issues of the press, calls for the exercise in a wide field of talents and acquirements. They come forth, for instance, in the stately quarterly, the less voluminous and dignified monthly, the lively weekly, and the rapid and dashing daily, which is required to photograph the hurrying hour, catching its changing views ere they fly. He whose capabilities have placed him in the front-rank of journalists, is fully competent to teach seven-tenths of all the college professors in the United States. Scholarships are good indeed, when applied to general education ; but the *art, craft, and mysteries of journalism cannot be taught, within the confines of a college.*

We will here state, that we have prepared very elaborate notes in regard to the press, both of the City and State ; likewise, matters appertaining to journalism in general, with the view of giving them to the public at some future day.

Journalism, the press, editorship, the craft in general,

are fruitful topics. They must, however, be discussed here with brevity.

Knowing the objects of the craft, and the probabilities within their aim, we find that there are many who may ascend the editorial *fauteuil.* Of the dignity and authority of that chair, we have already spoken. Some will attain the highly responsible position of business manager of the press; others again, will rise to stations of equally great responsibility, implying large capabilities; as, for instance, the foremanship, and thus the efforts of the entire craft are being strained according to the personal ambition of its respective members, to win the proud position of a public journalist. But to obtain success, what is most required? We answer diligence, industry, propriety of conduct, sobriety of habits, and assiduous study. If these conditions are complied with, success is assured to all.

> "Stet liber hic donec fluctus formica marinos
> Ebibat; et totum testudo perambulet orbem."

THE END.